NEW DIRECTIONS FOR TEACHING AN[...]

Robert J. Menges, *Northwestern University*
EDITOR-IN-CHIEF

Marilla D. Svinicki, *University of Texas, Austin*
ASSOCIATE EDITOR

Promoting Diversity in College Classrooms: Innovative Responses for the Curriculum, Faculty, and Institutions

Maurianne Adams
University of Massachusetts, Amherst

EDITOR

Number 52, Winter 1992

JOSSEY-BASS PUBLISHERS
San Francisco

PROMOTING DIVERSITY IN COLLEGE CLASSROOMS: INNOVATIVE RESPONSES
FOR THE CURRICULUM, FACULTY, AND INSTITUTIONS
Maurianne Adams (ed.)
New Directions for Teaching and Learning, no. 52
Robert J. Menges, Editor-in-Chief
Marilla D. Svinicki, Associate Editor

Microfilm copies of issues and articles are available in 16mm and 35mm,
as well as microfiche in 105mm, through University Microfilms Inc., 300
North Zeeb Road, Ann Arbor, Michigan 48106.

LC 85-644763   ISSN 0271-0633   ISBN 1-55542-745-6

NEW DIRECTIONS FOR TEACHING AND LEARNING is part of The Jossey-Bass
Higher and Adult Education Series and is published quarterly by Jossey-
Bass Inc., Publishers, 350 Sansome Street, San Francisco, California
94104-1310. Second-class postage paid at San Francisco, California, and at
additional mailing offices. POSTMASTER: Send address changes to New
Directions for Teaching and Learning, Jossey-Bass Inc., Publishers, 350
Sansome Street, San Francisco, California 94104-1310.

SUBSCRIPTIONS for 1992 cost $45.00 for individuals and $60.00 for institutions, agencies, and libraries.

EDITORIAL CORRESPONDENCE should be sent to Robert J. Menges, Northwestern University, Center for the Teaching Professions, 2003 Sheridan
Road, Evanston, Illinois 60208-2610.

Cover photograph by Richard Blair/Color & Light © 1990.

Contents

EDITOR'S NOTES

Those who dare to teach must never cease to learn.
—Brown, 1990

The writers for this volume start out with the assumption that the social and cultural diversity of the nation's population and work force is an established demographic fact rather than a debatable proposition. We further assume, as did the writers for our companion volume, *Teaching for Diversity* (Border and Chism, 1992), that the social and cultural diversity already within colleges and universities calls for significant changes in essentially conservative and predominantly monocultural curricula, teaching practices, and institutional characteristics. For those readers who may not be familiar with the range of arguments already brought forward by proponents of change, it may prove useful to summarize here the ethical and pragmatic views surveyed in the companion volume, namely: (1) the Moral Argument: there is a need to redress grievances of underrepresented social groups who have been unjustifiably denied access to higher education in this country; (2) the Demographic Argument: as the traditional pool of white applicants for higher education decreases and the pool of students of color increases, it is in the long-term, pragmatic self-interest of institutions of higher education to adjust the balance within their student populations; (3) the Civic Argument: the country's need for a skilled work force requires access to higher education for all citizens; (4) the Enrichment Argument: the intellectual enterprise is enhanced by the dialogue of multiple viewpoints; and (5) the Political Argument: inaction in the face of increasing campus conflict and violence is untenable. Access for students from underrepresented groups must be increased and appropriate support furnished.

However obvious it may be that social and cultural diversity is one of the most urgent challenges facing colleges and universities today, the issues it raises continue to divide college communities and to polarize intelligent and well-meaning faculty, students, and administrators around complex questions with no easy answers. The special difficulties appear to have two basic sources. One is the fundamental civic context for higher education in a nation whose paradoxical motto, *E pluribus unum,* contains deep contradictions. On the one hand, this motto has been taken by some to promise individual opportunity and personal freedom in exchange for a single overarching national identity, with public higher education the means of assimilation and access to the professional careers and individual living standards implied by the American dream. On the other hand, the promised opportunities have not been equitably provided for members of targeted social and cultural groups, of whom some may have assimilated into the broader culture but more remain outside, denied power and influence proportionate to their citizenship and their numbers.

A second special challenge comes from within higher education's shared traditions of discourse, communities of inquiry, and models of research and teaching, which taken together constitute a largely unexamined cultural legacy into which most of today's college faculty and administrators have been socialized. This academic culture can no longer be taken to stand for neutrality or objectivity or universality, so much as for the hegemony of a dominant strand of Western values, which constitute for differently socialized groups more an obstacle course than a stepping-stone to economic equity and political justice.

As the diversity debate continues, what we now understand to be the increasing ethnic diversity of the nation's population—projected at 24 percent Latino, 15 percent African American, and 12 percent Asian American by the year 2080—may well come to be viewed as relative homogeneity from a twenty-first-century perspective (Cortès, 1991). In Chapter Six of this volume, Curtis and Herrington make the point that for the majorities in their classes of second-language English speakers—immigrants and children of immigrants and first-generation college students—"multiculturalism is their culture" (p. 180). The multicultural curricula described in this volume characterize a step toward curricular change nationwide, as suggested by a recent survey that indicates that one-third to one-half of all colleges contacted already have some proportion of multicultural general education requirements, ethnic or gender studies programs, departmental offerings, advising programs, student and faculty recruitment efforts (Levine and Cureton, 1992). Thus this volume assumes that if change may seem slow, it is also incremental, already well underway, made up of small steps taken in different institutional settings—a process of trial and error for which, given our complex, conservative, decentralized collegiate systems, there may be few alternatives.

This volume takes up where the earlier volume, *Teaching for Diversity,* left off but retains the focus of the "New Directions in Teaching and Learning" sourcebooks on the classroom and the campus context for the classroom. Organized into three main sections, it presents several new perspectives on teaching practice in Part One, descriptive and narrative accounts of curricular and teaching innovations in Part Two, and a range of shared learnings from public university, community college, and private college multicultural change processes in Part Three.

Part One, "New Perspectives on Teaching and Learning," opens with an overview of multicultural teaching and learning, in which Marchesani and I comment on some issues that emerge as college faculty think about the diversity of their students in relation to their own cultural beliefs and academic values, and as they continue to develop more inclusive curricula and flexible repertoires of teaching strategies. Some of the points noted in Chapter One are elaborated elsewhere in the volume, notably in Chapters Two, Three, Five, Six, and Seven. In Chapter Two, Hardiman and Jackson discuss the process of developing one's racial identity and suggest some ways in which understanding the stages of that development can illuminate campus and classroom racial interactions. In Chapter Three, Weinstein and Obear acknowledge the highly charged, often volatile nature of bias issues in the classroom and the anticipatory fears and anxieties faculty understandably feel. They also discuss some useful strategies and emergency procedures for avoiding catastrophic thinking and alleviating stressful classroom situations.

Part Two, "Social Diversity in the Curriculum," presents a number of curricular themes and course-specific examples. In Chapter Four, Noronha ponders the differences, the parallels, and the interconnections between international and multicultural education and suggests several cross-cultural teaching strategies common to both. Her points are illustrated elsewhere in this volume, notably Chapters Five, Six, Eight, and Nine. In Chapter Five, Schmitz notes that in the absence of campus consensus, it falls to individual faculty to discover how to engage differences in the classroom. She provides numerous instances of curricular and pedagogical innovations at various institutions throughout the country. Several of her examples illustrate the partnership of global pluralism and domestic diversity that Noronha argued for in her chapter. Chapter Six describes the evolution of a writing curriculum for the students of which internationalism and multiculturalism are common denominators. In relation to those students, the authors, Curtis and Herrington, acknowledge their own cultural and generational distance: "Were we, as two Anglo women, traditionally educated and middle class, to select their readings and writings out of our background or out of the traditional composition reader canon to which we had become habituated, we would have created a curriculum in our image perhaps, in the university's image certainly, but decidedly not in theirs" (p. 75). Chapter Seven describes a cross-disciplinary general education social diversity course, whose goals include intergroup understanding, knowledge about specific manifestations of prejudice, experiential learning, and cross-cultural competencies of the sort generally identified in Chapters Five and Eight.

Part Three, "Social Diversity on College Campuses," presents a series of change agent lessons learned within the public and private, research university and community college sectors of higher education. In Chapter Eight, Hunt, Bell, Wei, and Ingle—faculty and staff from three public universities—discuss some common ground in their experiences of faculty development and curricular and institutional change, noting some impediments as well as supports for change within large, complex public institutions. In Chapter Nine, Jenrette and Adams present two snapshots of responses to diversity within two community colleges with different histories and community contexts. LaBare and Lang discuss parallels and variations between two dramatically different private colleges in Chapter Ten, with vignettes of institutional change and transformation at several stages of an ongoing evolutionary process.

All the writers in this volume acknowledge that terminology and language are deeply implicated in our diversity and multicultural debates. While noting inherent problems and limitations in our selection, we have tried throughout this volume to be consistent, using language that is clear in its context, neither pejorative nor inaccurate, reflecting difficulties in U.S. census classifications vis-à-vis changing demographics, and acknowledging names preferred by those so identified. Our attention throughout this volume to questions of race, ethnicity, and culture led us to rely on ethnic or cultural usage, such as *African American* or *European-heritage,* in that such terms parallel names for other ethnic groups by focusing attention on identities shared among peoples of common ancestry and descent. We used *people of color* to designate all nonwhite peoples and restricted *majority* and *minority* or *underrepresented* to draw attention only to specific classroom or collegiate social group proportions. Chapters that deal with questions of social justice as well as social diversity use the terms *dominant* and *targeted* to suggest unequal societal intergroup relationships. By *targeted* we refer throughout this volume to members of social and cultural groups who are targets of individual prejudice as well as institutional and cultural discrimination, specifically, African American, Asian American, Latino, and Native American students; all women, gay, lesbian, or bisexual students; students with a range of physical or mental disabilities; Jewish and other "minority" cultural and religious groups that have historically been denied access and experienced hostility and harassment on American college campuses. We use terms of color (*Black* and *White*) in chapters in which racism on the basis of color is the major issue under consideration.

Among the many colleagues, students, and friends who have contributed in important ways to this volume, I want to express special gratitude to Laura Border, Barbara Burn, and Nancy Chism for assistance in identifying authors; to Robert Bureau and Mary McClintock for resourceful and meticulous library research; to Paulette Dalpes, Arlyn Diamond, and Mary Deane Sorcinelli for valuable editorial comment; to Darrin Alves for technical assistance; and to John A. Hunt for perceptive and resilient editorial, collegial, and personal support.

Maurianne Adams
Editor

References

Border, L.L.B., and Chism, N.V.N. "Editor's Notes." In L.L.B. Border and N.V.N. Chism (eds.), *Teaching for Diversity*. New Directions for Teaching and Learning, no. 49. San Francisco: Jossey-Bass, 1992.

Brown, T. J. "The Impact of Culture on Cognition." *Clearing House for the Contemporary Educator in Middle and Secondary Schools,* 1990, *63* (7), 305–309.

Cortès, C. E. "Pluribus & Unum: The Quest for Community amid Diversity." *Change,* 1991, *23* (5), 8–16.

Levine, A., and Cureton, J. "The Quiet Revolution: Eleven Facts About Multiculturalism and the Curriculum." *Change,* 1992, *24* (1), 25–29.

MAURIANNE ADAMS is a faculty member in the Social Justice Education Program and the Human Development Program, School of Education, and associate director of Residential Academic Programs at the University of Massachusetts, Amherst.

PART ONE

New Perspectives on Teaching and Learning

This chapter brings together the dimensions of teaching and learning that have particular relevance to social and cultural diversity in college classrooms—students, instructor, course content, and teaching methods.

Dynamics of Diversity in the Teaching-Learning Process: A Faculty Development Model for Analysis and Action

Linda S. Marchesani, Maurianne Adams

The social and cultural composition of today's college student population differs markedly from that of thirty years ago, when many of today's senior faculty were beginning their teaching careers and younger faculty were still in school or college. The traditional schooling of college faculty has ill prepared many of us for the social and cultural diversity of today's students, a diversity that may differ across geographic areas or within the public or private, research or teaching, secular or denominational institutions that taken together constitute American higher education.

These changes in student populations have resulted from factors familiar to us all, primarily the educational equity efforts of the 1960s. Federal intervention to remove barriers, changes in overall national demographic and immigration patterns, and greater variability in the sequencing of higher education in relation to family and work have led to classrooms populated by women; students of color; older, part-time, and international students; as well as students with various disabilities and a range of sexual orientations (WICHE, 1991; Carter and Wilson, 1991). So it is not surprising that faculty find themselves maintaining an unexamined academic culture while facing multicultural challenges from students of underrepresented racial, ethnic, and linguistic backgrounds, by women questioning the dominant cultural mode, by older adults returning to formal schooling from family or occupational experiences. The understandable difficulty for faculty socialized within another his-

NEW DIRECTIONS FOR TEACHING AND LEARNING, no. 52, Winter 1992   © Jossey-Bass Publishers

torical and cultural situation is to know how best to facilitate diverse student learning within an increasingly multicultural context. That difficulty can lead faculty into the stance of seeming to argue for academic standards while they unwittingly transmit a heretofore unexamined culture.

Although increasing diversification of American higher education is forecast well into the twenty-first century, several additional disturbing trends give further cause for concern (Gerald and Hussar, 1991; *One Third of a Nation*, 1988):

African American, Latino, and Native American high school completion rates, college participation, and degree attainment continue to be lower than white rates (Carter and Wilson, 1991; *Focus on Blacks*, 1992; *Focus on Hispanics*, 1991; *Focus on American Indian . . .*, 1991; Smith, 1989).

Although women constitute the majority of students in higher education and their educational advancement at every level continues to rise, women are grossly underrepresented in the mathematical and scientific fields, and the economic return for a college education is greater for men than for women (Touchton and Davis, 1991).

The literature on all nonmainstream populations in higher education describes a continued host of personal and institutional barriers facing students from nontraditional backgrounds (Smith, 1989).

What these trends tell us is that we have not yet learned how to maximize educational opportunities and minimize or remove educational barriers for large numbers of our current and future college students in our classes and institutional life.

We acknowledge that the achievement of a truly multicultural college environment involves large-scale, complex, sustained organizational and cultural transformation (Smith, 1989; Jackson and Holvino, 1986, 1988). No dimension of that goal seems more elusive, however, than the critical analysis of the teaching and learning enterprise that exists at the heart of higher education purposes. We have attempted in this chapter to present a way for faculty to organize the often complicated task of understanding the ingredients of teaching and learning as these occur within a socially and culturally diverse college classroom. We present a model (Jackson, 1988) that singles out four dimensions of teaching and learning as distinct domains, which for the purposes of this chapter are addressed separately, even though in real life they are almost always difficult to disentangle.

The four dimensions of teaching and learning that appear to have particular relevance to issues of social and cultural diversity (see Figure 1) are (1) students: knowing one's students and understanding the ways that students from various social and cultural backgrounds experience the college classroom; (2) instructor: knowing oneself as a person with a

Figure 1.1. Dynamics of Multicultural Teaching and Learning

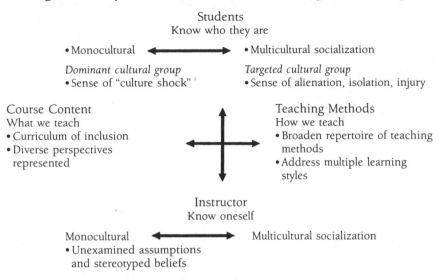

Source: Adapted from Jackson, 1988.

prior history of academic socialization interacting with a social and cultural background and learned beliefs; (3) course content: creating a curriculum that incorporates diverse social and cultural perspectives; (4) teaching methods: developing a broad repertoire of teaching methods to address learning styles of students from different social backgrounds more effectively.

Students: Know Who They Are

In order to understand better the implications of the increased social and cultural diversity of our students, it helps to examine the ways in which students from different social and cultural groups experience the classroom environment. Mainstream students, often coming from homogeneous home and school communities, may experience a kind of culture shock as they encounter diverse populations and multicultural course content in some of their classes. Students from targeted social groups, in some cases also coming from fairly monocultural home or school communities and often the first college generation from working-class or recent immigrant families, may find their classroom experiences characterized by cultural isolation, tokenism, and potential alienation.

Although there are adjustment dilemmas common to both groups of students, mainstream as well as targeted, our emphasis in this section is on targeted students, for whom the college classroom is too often a place of cultural isolation and of norms, values, and customs that contradict their home socializations, and the curriculum too often represents a male perspective on the accomplishments of Western civilization. Targeted students can be isolated from their peers because their status as a classroom minority makes them both more and less visible and vulnerable to stereotypic comments, thoughtless assumptions, and casual jokes (Evans and Wall, 1991; Smith, 1989; Pearson, Shavlick, and Touchton, 1989; Wright, 1987).

Alienated. Recent inquiry into multicultural teaching and learning has focused on reframing the classroom environment as one that is not, as has been claimed, culture or value neutral, but that results from and reflects the cultural norms and traditions established by its predominantly Western male originators (Adams, 1992; Kuh and Whitt, 1988; Condon, 1986). Traditionally sanctioned individual performance, reasoned argumentation, impersonal objectivity, and sports-like competitiveness represent a distinct set of cultural norms and values that, for many students, are at best culturally unfamiliar and at worst contradict the norms and values of their gender or of their racial or ethnic backgrounds. For example, Asian American students find themselves in a bicultural dilemma if they have been socialized to affirm modesty, cooperation, and nonassertiveness in their family and community but are expected to be assertive or competitive in the classroom. Faculty can become more knowledgeable about and sensitive to the values and beliefs of students from diverse racial and cultural groups, while also not assuming that all students have experienced the same socialization in their homes or communities and taking care not to create or perpetuate new stereotypes.

In addition, students from diverse social backgrounds may respond differently to the powerful implicit messages about what bodies of knowledge are worth studying and which individual contributors worth acknowledging that the established college curriculum communicates. A curriculum that is limited to the traditions, values, and contributions of Western civilization may convey to students that African American or Native American history and traditions or the achievements of women are not an important part of the educational agenda.

Isolated. When students are part of a numerical minority in college classrooms, they often experience the effects of tokenism—increased visibility, scrutiny, and pressure to perform (Smith, 1989). Unlike their mainstream counterparts, students of color and students with disabilities, for example, may stand out among their teachers and peers whatever their behaviors, whether outspoken or silent, whether on time for class or absent. During classroom discussions, such students are often unwittingly solicited as spokespersons for their group on particular issues, apparently on the assumption that everyone from a particular racial or ethnic group thinks alike and furthermore that their expertise in class is limited to their group's perspective. Being made the unwelcome center of attention when topics of race, culture, gender, religion, sexual orientation, age, or disabilities are discussed but generally ignored otherwise creates for students the paradox of visibility/invisibility, which can isolate them and lead them to withdraw, thereby limiting their participation and jeopardizing their academic success.

Students from groups outside the traditional academic mainstream describe not only the experience of heightened visibility but also feeling invisible, excluded, and ignored by faculty and fellow students. During the formation of discussion and study groups, for example, students with disabilities may be initially excluded and cut off from valuable learning opportunities as well as social interaction. Women and students of color may be overlooked, given less time to respond to questions, interrupted more frequently, and not acknowledged or validated in the same ways as their European American male counterparts (Sandler and Hall, 1982; Sandler, 1987).

Injured. Students' sense of pride and self-esteem can be injured by demeaning stereotypes, insensitive jokes, derogatory comments, and thoughtless language and actions on the part of faculty and fellow students. Negative assumptions about intellectual competence and qualifications ("You're here because of affirmative action"), lowering standards or expressing surprise at good performance ("That's a great paper for a black student"), as well as positive expectations founded on group membership rather than personal interests (all Asian students are good at math or science, all Latino students excel in drama or the arts) can be acted on and internalized by students and contribute to a cycle of damaging self-fulfilling prophesies.

Instructor: Know Oneself

Our faculty development model asks that as faculty we focus thoughtful attention on our own beliefs and attitudes, as derived not only from our academic socialization but also from our individual experiences of a particular social and cultural background with specific values and beliefs. In this effort, we need to assess our comfort and skills in various cross-cultural situations, take responsibility for obtaining knowledge about the cultural backgrounds of our students, and become more aware of the impact of our socialization and learned beliefs on our interactions with students whose social and cultural backgrounds differ from our own (Cones, Noonan, and Jahna, 1983; Chapter Three, this volume).

As a society we are only one generation removed from legally sanctioned educational segregation, and many faculty grew up or are currently living in monocultural home, educational, and community environments. Prior monocultural experiences may lead to discomfort in unfamiliar multicultural environments. More significant than discomfort, however, is having been socialized with an unexamined set of traditions, beliefs, and assumptions about ourselves and a limited knowledge about others (Bowser and Hunt, 1981; Cones, Noonan, and Jahna, 1983; Katz, 1978). Furthermore, the monocultural experiences of faculty from dominant groups socialized within mainstream culture often create a context in which attitudes, beliefs, and behaviors are not acknowledged as reflections of a particular racial group (white), ethnic heritage (European), or gender orientation (male) but are thought of as universal human traits (Sandler, 1987). The tendency of individuals from dominant cultural groups to see their norms and traditions as universally valued and preferred supports a cultural embeddedness that makes it extremely difficult to acknowledge the extent of negative assumptions and stereotypes toward those with other educational values or beliefs. Although we are not responsible for the culture-specific beliefs we grew up with, we are surely responsible for examining and questioning them as adults and as educators.

Curriculum: What We Teach

The curriculum, or what we teach, is typically the major focus for discussion and debate by college faculty. The current movement toward diversity and multiculturalism has rekindled that debate with an intensity that has not been seen since the development of racial and ethnic studies and women's studies in the early 1970s (Levine, 1992; Butler and Walter, 1991; "Curricular and Institutional Change," 1990). It is beyond the scope of this chapter to enter into the debate as such. One especially relevant question, however, is the extent to which curriculum reform is a part of multicultural education and the kinds of change most effective for creating a curriculum that reflects a range of social perspectives. Within the context of the larger debate, some authors take the position that a "curriculum of inclusion" is critical for educating all students to live in a socially diverse society and an increasingly interdependent world (Gaff, 1992; Butler, 1991; Higgenbotham, 1990). Our four-part model identifies the curriculum—what we teach—as an inescapable area for attention as we engage in a developmental process from exclusion to inclusion. We must ask ourselves as faculty to examine the perspectives previously used and to develop curricula so that the course content (themes and issues), the course materials (texts and assignments), and the sources of knowledge (theorists and authorities) we validate and emphasize reach beyond the current European traditions of thought and male authorities to include the contributions, experiences, and perspectives of the traditionally marginalized but increasingly visible members of society.

We have found the transformation phase model described below useful in that it is based on actual experiences of curriculum change in women's and ethnic studies, and its several phases represent qualitatively distinctive modes by which faculty gradually reexperience the curriculum of their specific disciplines through an "inside-out approach" and from the multiple perspectives of the previously excluded (Schuster and Van Dyne, 1985; Green, 1989).

Mode 1: The Exclusive Curriculum. The experiences and perspectives that characterize this curriculum are those of the mainstream academic disciplines, still largely male and derived from European academic values. This tradition tends not to incorporate alternative perspectives or seems to present them in ways that devalue their contributions or present their experiences in stereotypic or demeaning ways.

Mode 2: The Exceptional Outsider. This curricular mode includes contributions of exceptional individuals from marginalized groups, on traditional criteria. The new perspectives they offer do not result in reconceptualizing the field of study. Although it is decidedly incomplete, this mode of reform enables students from underrepresented racial, cultural, and other social groups at least to feel included in the subject of study, and enables dominant students to broaden their reference points.

Mode 3: Understanding the Outsider. This dimension of curricular reform goes beyond including exceptional individuals in the margins of an otherwise unaltered curriculum and is characterized instead by efforts to analyze and understand the reasons for and conditions of exclusion for nonmainstream groups. Differences in culture or gender are still viewed in relation to the dominant ideas and contributions of those that have traditionally set standards and defined norms of participation. Critical examination of those norms and standards at this point tend to focus on how to equalize the playing field rather than on fundamentally changing the rules of the game.

Mode 4: Getting Inside the Outsider. In this mode, the authentic voices and experiences of the former "outsiders" are considered directly and in their own terms rather than interpreted through the lenses of the dominant culture. Varied voices help make clear the multiple nature of reality as it is perceived from the inside out, and these diverse voices are valued for what they can tell us about various perspectives on reality.

Mode 5: The Transformed Curriculum. This approach eliminates the unexamined assumption of cultural hegemony that was established by the exclusive curriculum and replaces it with a curriculum that acknowledges the new knowledge and new scholarship that is created when the experiences, perspectives, and worldviews of traditionally marginalized peoples are taken as multiple centers in the curriculum. It encourages new ways of thinking and incorporates new methodologies, so that different epistemological questions are raised, old assumptions are questioned, subjective data sources are considered, and prior theories either revised or invalidated. Finally, the curriculum of inclusion is complete when new ways of teaching and learning accompany the transformed curriculum (Green, 1989; Border and Chism, 1992; Butler and Walter, 1991; Chapter Six, this volume).

Teaching Methods: How We Teach

The fourth dimension of this model—the *how* as distinct from the *what* of teaching—addresses a frequently overlooked component of the multicultural classroom dialogue, the complex interplay between social and cultural worldview on the one hand and teaching or learning style on the other. Typically, many college faculty teach the way they were taught and thereby replicate unexamined teaching practices characterized by requiring the acquisition of course content and disciplinary knowledge, the transmission of information via the lecture as the method of choice, and the evaluation of achievement as demonstrated solely by individual performance (Kuh and Whitt, 1988). These traditionally sanctioned academic practices are no longer viewed as culturally neutral but as reflective of an implicit or "hidden" curriculum, neither familiar nor welcoming to students whose previous school, home, and community socialization has valued different norms and behavioral expectations (Adams, 1992; Green, 1989; Condon, 1986). The result is that women students, students of color, and students from linguistic minorities in particular are often faced with bicultural dilemmas as they strive to balance the behavioral expectations of college classes (assertion, competition, independence, and individualism) with their own cultural norms and values. If they do not succeed, they are often misunderstood as underprepared, unmotivated, or unintelligent (Pearson, Shavlick, and Touchton, 1989; Hale-Benson, 1986; Ramirez and Castaneda, 1974).

Effective teaching in the multicultural classroom depends on the teacher's willingness and ability to develop a flexible repertoire of teaching strategies so as to maximize the match between the cultural and learning styles of students. This in turn calls for information concerning the cultural orientation that students, understood both as individuals and as members of distinct social groups, may bring with them to the college classroom. The broad findings in cultural and learning style studies of the development, socialization, and schooling of African, Asian, and Native Americans, Latinos, and women suggest some important areas where faculty might consider utilizing alternative teaching modes (Anderson and Adams, 1992; Tharp, 1989; Shade, 1989; Pearson, Shavlick, and Touchton, 1989). These alternatives include collaborative and cooperative learning activities to balance traditions of individualistic competition; visual, auditory, or dramatic demonstrations as alternatives to the exclusive use of verbal explanation and written expression; group, peer and cross-age learning projects as well as individual questions and answers; study groups and group projects built on peer relationships instead of exclusively solo study; active learning projects, simulations, and role plays to balance the passive learnings of the lecture-and-listen note-taking mode.

Various instructional design models and pedagogical guides are available to faculty who wish to test new alternatives gradually (Weinstein, 1988; Palmer, 1981; Pfeiffer and Jones, 1974). The Learning Style Manual (Smith and Kolb, 1986) and teaching models based on Kolb's Learning Style Inventory (Svinicki and Dixon, 1987; Anderson and Adams, 1992) can provide ideas that will help faculty plan to utilize teaching modes unfamiliar to them and ultimately to stretch the stylistic resources of their teaching repertoire.

As we enlarge our repertoire of curricular and teaching strategies, we increase the likelihood of academic success for a broader range of students and we enable more socially diverse college students to feel welcomed, included, and competent. The benefits of instructional flexibility, however, extend to the *traditional student* as well, because varied teaching is effective teaching in any event. It increases the likelihood of matching learning differences for all students, while providing regular practice and development in their less preferred modes. Finally, a college teacher's repertoire of teaching strategies exemplifies for all students the multicultural value of reciprocity rather than the monocultural expectation of acculturation.

In conclusion, we believe this four-part model of the dynamics of multicultural teaching and learning may prove useful to faculty and in faculty development programs. We propose three applications. First, the model can be used by the college teacher as a framework, organizer, and diagnostic tool for his or her own classroom experience. Second, it serves as a framework for the single workshops or faculty development series suggested by the faculty development literature (Schmitz, Paul, and Greenberg, 1992; Butler and Schmitz, 1991; Paige-Pointer and Auletta, 1990). Third, it can help to systematize and manage the extensive new literature that is emerging from the dialogue about multiculturalism currently underway in American higher education.

References

Adams, M. "Cultural Inclusion in the American College Classroom." In L.L.B. Border and N.V.N. Chism (eds.), *Teaching for Diversity.* New Directions for Teaching and Learning, no. 49. San Francisco: Jossey-Bass, 1992.

Anderson, J. A., and Adams, M. "Acknowledging the Learning Styles of Diverse Student Populations: Implications for Instructional Design." In L.L.B. Border and N.V.N. Chism (eds.), *Teaching for Diversity.* New Directions for Teaching and Learning, no. 49. San Francisco: Jossey-Bass, 1992.

Border, L.L.B., and Chism, N.V.N. (eds.). *Teaching for Diversity.* New Directions for Teaching and Learning, no. 49. San Francisco: Jossey-Bass, 1992.

Bowser, B. P., and Hunt, R. G. (eds.). *Impact of Racism on White Americans.* Newbury Park, Calif.: Sage, 1981.

Butler, J. E. "The Difficult Dialogue of Curriculum Transformation: Ethnic Studies and Women's Studies." In J. E. Butler and J. C. Walter (eds.), *Transforming the Curriculum: Ethnic Studies and Women's Studies.* Albany: State University of New York Press, 1991.

Butler, J. E., and Schmitz, B. "Different Voices: A Model Institute for Integrating Women of Color into Undergraduate American Literature and History Courses." In J. E. Butler and J. C. Walter (eds.), *Transforming the Curriculum: Ethnic Studies and Women's Studies.* Albany: State University of New York Press, 1991.

Butler, J. E., and Walter, J. C. (eds.). *Transforming the Curriculum: Ethnic Studies and Women's Studies.* Albany: State University of New York Press, 1991.

Carter, D. J., and Wilson, R. *Ninth Annual Status Report on Minorities in Higher Education.* Washington, D.C.: American Council on Education, 1991.

Condon, J. C. "The Ethnocentric Classroom." In J. M. Civikly (ed.), *Communicating in College Classrooms.* New Directions in Teaching and Learning, no. 26. San Francisco: Jossey-Bass, 1986.

Cones, J. H., Noonan, J. F., and Jahna, D. (eds.). *Teaching Minority Students.* New Directions for Teaching and Learning, no. 16. San Francisco: Jossey-Bass, 1983.

"Curricular and Institutional Change." *Women's Studies Quarterly,* 1990, *18* (1, 2). Special issue.

Evans, N. J., and Wall, V. A. *Beyond Tolerance: Gays, Lesbians and Bisexuals on Campus.* Alexandria, Va.: American College Personnel Association, 1991.

Focus on American Indian/Alaska Natives. Ethnic Report. Washington, D.C.: National Education Association, Human and Civil Rights, Oct. 1991.

Focus on Blacks. Ethnic Report. Washington, D.C.: National Education Association, Human and Civil Rights, Feb. 1992.

Focus on Hispanics. Ethnic Report. Washington, D.C.: National Education Association, Human and Civil Rights, Dec. 1991.

Gaff, J. G. "Beyond Politics: The Educational Issues Inherent in Multicultural Education." *Change,* 1992, *24* (1), 30–36.

Gerald, D. E., and Hussar, W. J. *Projections of Education Statistics to 2002.* Washington, D.C.: National Center for Education Statistics, U.S. Department of Education, 1991. (NCES 91-490)

Green, M. F. (ed.). *Minorities on Campus: A Handbook for Enhancing Diversity.* Washington, D.C.: American Council on Education, 1989.

Hale-Benson, J. E. *Black Children: Their Roots, Culture, and Learning Style.* (Rev. ed.) Baltimore, Md.: Johns Hopkins University Press, 1986.

Higgenbotham, E. "Designing an Inclusive Curriculum: Bringing All Women into the Core." *Women's Studies Quarterly,* 1990, *18* (1, 2), 7–23.

Jackson, B. W. "A Model for Teaching to Diversity." Unpublished paper from faculty and teaching assistant development workshop, University of Massachusetts, Amherst, October 1988.

Jackson, B. W., and Holvino, E. "Working with Multicultural Organizations: Matching Theory and Practice." In M. R. Donleavy (ed.), *Conference Proceedings of the 1986 Organizational Conference.* New York: Organizational Development Network, 1986.

Jackson, B. W., and Holvino, E. "Developing Multicultural Organizations." *Creative Change: Journal of Religion and the Applied Behavioral Sciences,* 1988, *9* (2), 14–19.

Katz, J. H. *White Awareness: Handbook for Anti-Racism Training.* Norman: University of Oklahoma Press, 1978.

Kuh, G. D., and Whitt, E. J. *The Invisible Tapestry: Culture in American Colleges and Universities.* ASHE-ERIC Higher Education Reports, no. 1. Washington, D.C.: Association for the Study of Higher Education, 1988.

Levine, A. (ed.). "The Curriculum and Multiculturalism." *Change,* 1992, *24* (1). Special issue.

One Third of a Nation: A Report of the Commission on Minority Participation in Education and American Life. Washington, D.C.: American Council on Education, 1988.

Paige-Pointer, B., and Auletta, G. S. "Restructuring the Curriculum: Barriers and Bridges." *Women's Studies Quarterly,* 1990, *18* (1, 2), 86–95.

Palmer, A. B. "Learning Cycles: Models of Behavior Change." In J. E. Jones and J. W. Pfeiffer (eds.), *The 1981 Annual Handbook for Group Facilitators.* San Diego: University Associates, 1981.

Pearson, C. S., Shavlick, D. L., and Touchton, J. G. (eds.). *Educating the Majority: Women Challenge Tradition in Higher Education.* New York: American Council on Education/Macmillan, 1989.

Pfeiffer, J. W., and Jones, J. E. (eds.). *Handbook of Structured Experiences for Human Relations Training.* Vols. 1 and 2. La Jolla, Calif.: University Associates, 1974.

Ramirez, M., and Castaneda, A. *Cultural Democracy, Bicognitive Development, and Education.* New York: Academic Press, 1974.

Sandler, B. "The Classroom Climate: Still a Chilly One for Women." In C. Lasser (ed.), *Educating Men and Women Together: Coeducation in a Changing World.* Champaign, Ill.: University of Illinois Press, 1987.

Sandler, B., and Hall, R. M. *The Classroom Climate: A Chilly One for Women?* Washington, D.C.: Association of American Colleges, 1982.

Schmitz, B., Paul, S. P., and Greenberg, J. D. "Creating Multicultural Classrooms: An Experience-Derived Faculty Development Program." In L.L.B. Border and N.V.N. Chism (eds.), *Teaching for Diversity.* New Directions for Teaching and Learning, no. 49. San Francisco: Jossey-Bass, 1992.

Schuster, M. R., and Van Dyne, S. R. *Women's Place in the Academy: Transforming the Liberal Arts Curriculum.* Totowa, N.J.: Rowman & Allanheld, 1985.

Shade, B. J. (ed.). *Culture, Style, and the Educative Process.* Springfield, Ill.: Thomas, 1989.

Smith, D. G. *The Challenge of Diversity: Involvement or Alienation in the Academy?* ASHE-ERIC Higher Education Reports, no. 5. Washington, D.C.: Association for the Study of Higher Education, 1989.

Smith, D. M., and Kolb, D. A. *User's Guide for the Learning Style Inventory.* Boston: McBer, 1986.

Svinicki, M. D., and Dixon, N. M. "The Kolb Model Modified for Classroom Activities." *College Teaching,* 1987, *35* (4), 141–146.

Tharp, R. F. "Psychocultural Variables and Constants: Effects on Teaching and Learning in Schools." *American Psychologist,* 1989, *44* (2), 349–359.

Touchton, J. G., and Davis, L. *Fact Book on Women in Higher Education.* New York: American Council on Education/Macmillan, 1991.

Weinstein, G. "Design Elements for Intergroup Awareness Training." *Journal for Specialists in Group Work,* 1988, *13* (2), 96–103.

WICHE: Western Interstate Commission for Higher Education. *The Road to College: Educational Progress by Race and Ethnicity.* Boulder, Colo.: Western Interstate Commission for Higher Education, 1991.

Wright, D. J. (ed.). *Responding to the Needs of Today's Minority Students.* New Directions for Student Services, no. 38. San Francisco: Jossey-Bass, 1987.

LINDA S. MARCHESANI is assistant director of Residential Academic Programs and adjunct faculty in the Social Justice Education Program, School of Education, University of Massachusetts, Amherst.

MAURIANNE ADAMS is a faculty member in the Social Justice Education Program and the Human Development Program, School of Education, and associate director of Residential Academic Programs, University of Massachusetts, Amherst.

Understanding the racial identity development process of Black and White Americans assists educators in making informed responses to challenging racial dynamics on college campuses.

Racial Identity Development: Understanding Racial Dynamics in College Classrooms and on Campus

Rita Hardiman, Bailey W. Jackson

In recent years, educators in higher education have paid increased attention to the ways that interactions among students from diverse social groups are manifested everywhere on campus. Of particular concern are the effects of these interactions on both the social and academic life of the campus community. It is apparent that these interactions are not what they could or should be. As the academy first tried to increase the numbers of students from underrepresented social groups and then established academic and social support programs, its efforts were divided between integration of socially diverse populations into the existing campus community and creation of shared multicultural communities that maintained the integrity of diverse social groups. Instead of expecting students from underrepresented social groups to conform to preexisting college norms, college faculty and administrators now seem to be open to the new perspectives and expectations these students bring with them to the campus and classroom (Levine, 1991). This shift in the understanding and definition of diversity could have significant implications for campus climate, student interactions, student personnel programming, and the curriculum.

It is useful to note that the most significant shift in the evolution of approaches to social diversity on campus can be described as a shift from asking *who* is on campus to understanding *how* each group views the world as a function of its experiences with social injustice and the influence of cultural orientation (Border and Chism, 1992; Jones, 1990; Jackson and Hardiman, 1988; Ho, 1987). It is clear to us that these two issues, which we differentiate for emphasis, are not only related but

indeed inseparable and must be factored in if we are to have any understanding of student identity. In other words, it is difficult if not impossible to understand group differences merely as differences in cultural
expression. We must also recognize that the various manifestations of
social oppression, such as racism, ethnocentrism, or sexism, have a
significant impact on the worldview, self-concept, self-esteem, and behavior of both those who benefit from the system of social oppression
(dominants) and those who are victims of this system (targets).

In this chapter we focus on the intersection of social diversity and
social justice at the individual level of personal belief, attitude, and
behavior, by presenting a model of racial identity development that
makes several assumptions: the identity development of both dominant
and targeted group members is influenced by White racism in the United
States; this identity development can be described as shifts in worldview
or consciousness in sequential stages; individual interactions within groups
as well as between groups are influenced by the developmental stage of
one's racial identity (Jackson, 1976a, 1976b; Hardiman, 1982). We understand *racial identity* to mean a sense of self in the context of one's
racial group membership, which includes all aspects of that group's
culture. Racial identity development theory "concerns the psychological
implications of racial group membership; that is, belief systems that
evolve in reaction to perceived differential racial group membership"
(Helms, 1990, p. 4; see also Cross, Parham, and Helms, in press; Abrams
and Hogg, 1990; Smith, 1991). We understand this perceived racial
group membership as developmental, in that, as with other developmental processes, one's racial identity changes over time to become more
congruent with one's range of experiences, personal beliefs, and other
dimensions of self-identity.

In the early 1970s, one of the authors pioneered in what has since
emerged as the field of racial identity development and, writing independently of Cross, developed the model of Black identity development that
closely resembles the model reported here (Jackson, 1976a, 1976b; Cross,
1971, 1978). Jackson's work was germinating during the latter years of the
contemporary civil rights movement and focused on how Black Americans
develop individual identities around their understanding of their Blackness—that is, their social group identification and affiliation within the
social context of racism. Both Jackson and Cross argued not only that Black
Americans constitute a distinct cultural group, but also that their cultural
group has experienced a history of systemic oppression as a racial minority.
Therefore, their individual identities as Blacks and as Americans are affected
both by Black culture and by American racism.

The work of Hardiman (1979), a colleague with Jackson at the
University of Massachusetts, became the first model of White identity
development, that is, the first model to describe how members of a

dominant racial identity group (Whites) develop a consciousness of racial identity.

This chapter will present a synthesis of both authors' evolving work on the development of racial identity in Black and White Americans. (We use the racial/color designators in this chapter, rather than the ethnic terms African American or European American, to highlight the "discrimination" rather than the "diversity" aspect of the interaction.) The racial identity development model will help teachers and administrators alike understand the developmental processes that Black and White students are undergoing (see Tatum, 1992; Mann and Moser, 1991) and, in fact, may assist faculty and staff in understanding their own racial identity processes. It describes how racism affects the development of a sense of group identity for Blacks and Whites by examining the increasingly conscious attention both dominant group members (Whites) and target group members (Blacks) experience as they struggle with racism and strive to attain liberated racial identities in a persistently racist environment. The authors are White and Black, respectively, and have each focused their research and writing on those two racial groups. However, the reader should not assume that we view racism as uniquely a Black-White issue. Racism in the United States affects all targeted racial groups as well as persons of mixed heritage. Other racial identity models are also available; see Kim (1981) for Asian Americans, Hayes-Bautista (1974) for Chicanos, and Wijeyesinghe (1992) for Black/White biracial identity factors. These racial identity development models can be viewed as road maps of the journey from an identity in which racism and domination are internalized to an identity that is affirming and liberated from racism. This road map highlights five major points of reference, each point descriptive of a stage or predominant mode of consciousness. *Stage* is a convenient metaphor for states of consciousness or worldviews that are developmental in nature and that change over time in response to experience and knowledge to become more complex and more adequate internal reference points for examining and understanding one's own beliefs, values, and behaviors.

We have named the five stages (1) *naive,* without consciousness of social identity; (2) *acceptance* of the prevailing social definitions of Blackness and Whiteness; (3) *resistance,* the rejection of the racist definition of Blackness and Whiteness; (4) *redefinition,* suggesting the renaming of one's racial identity; and (5) *internalization,* the integration of the redefined racial identity into all aspects of the self (see Figure 2.1). The acceptance and resistance stages are described in relation to two possible manifestations, passive (unconscious) or active (conscious). The stages of redefinition and internalization involve by their very nature, conscious, active choices and therefore have no passive-stage manifestations, whereas the naive stage is by definition not conscious.

Figure 2.1. Stages of Racial Identity Development

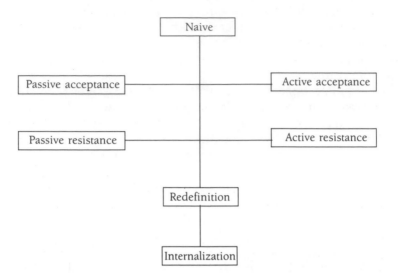

The transition from one stage to another usually occurs when an individual recognizes that his or her current worldview is either illogical or contradicted by new experience and information, detrimental to a healthy self-concept or no longer serving some important self-interest. During the transition periods, a person may appear to him or herself and to others to be in two stages simultaneously, for indeed they are exiting from one stage and entering the next stage at the same time.

The racial identity development model will be presented as follows in this section. There will be a general overview of the stage of development presented, to be followed by separate descriptions of the nature of each stage for a White person and a Black person.

Stage One—Naive

The naive stage of consciousness describes the consciousness of race in childhood, when there is little or no social awareness of race per se (Derman-Sparks, Higa, and Sparks, 1980). During this period members of both dominant groups and target groups are vulnerable to the logic system and worldview of their socializing agents (for example, parents, teachers, the media, and significant others). Children at this stage become aware of the physical differences and some obvious cultural differences between themselves and others, and while they may not feel completely comfortable with people who are different, they generally do not feel fearful, hostile, or either inferior or superior. They may display a curiosity about or an interest in understanding the differences between people, but they have not yet learned to see some differences as more normal, or correct, or valued than others in the social world. This stage generally covers the developmental period between birth and about four years of age.

In the transition from naive to acceptance, two related changes take place in the racial worldviews of both Blacks and Whites. One is that children begin to learn and adopt an ideology about their own racial group and as well as other racial groups. They internalize many covert and some overt messages, that being Black means being less than, that Whiteness equals superiority or normality, beauty, importance, and power. The second change is that members of both racial groups begin to learn that there are formal and informal rules, institutions, and authority figures that permit some behaviors and prohibit others, and that people encounter negative consequences for stepping out of these rules regarding how the races relate to each other.

Stage Two—Acceptance

The naive stage of consciousness is followed by a stage of acceptance. In one sense, the stage of acceptance represents the absorption, whether conscious or unconscious, of an ideology of racial dominance and subordination which touches upon all facets of personal and public life. A person at this stage has accepted the messages about racial group membership, the superiority of the dominant group members and the dominant culture, and the inferiority of target group people and cultures.

Acceptance Stage for Whites. For Whites in passive acceptance, there may not be any conscious identification with being White. Whiteness is taken for granted and seen as normal. Whites in passive acceptance are thus more subtly racist in perpetuating dominant beliefs and actions, because they are unable to see themselves as racists or as actively prejudiced people, whom they describe as being actively or vocally against targeted racial groups (such as the Ku Klux Klan). In this stage, White people may hold the following attitudes and beliefs:

That Blacks, Asians, Native Americans, and some Hispanics are "culturally deprived" and need help to learn how to assimilate into "American" or White society

That affirmative action is reverse discrimination, because people of color are being given opportunities that Whites have never had

That White culture (music, art, literature) is classical or high culture, whereas the culture of people of color is primitive, craft not art, and generally of lower class

Various stereotypes such as that Blacks are natural athletes, Hispanics are naturally violent, Asians are mysterious and have innate math abilities, and so on.

Whites in passive acceptance may engage in the following behaviors:

Excluding, avoiding, or ignoring people of color, because they are different or strange or not quite right
Patronizing behavior, such as being extra friendly and solicitous to people of color.

In contrast, Whites who move from the naive stage to the active acceptance stage tend to be more vocal and forthright in expressing their sense of White superiority. They may express consciousness of White identity and pride in being White. In the extreme form, people in this stage may actually join White supremacist organizations. The recent emergence of "White student unions" may be one contemporary example of this tendency. Various forms of racial harassment and acting out are also indicative of the active acceptance stage, made easier on college campuses by the influence of alcohol and peer pressure.

Acceptance Stage for Blacks. The Black person in the acceptance stage of consciousness follows the prevailing notion that "White is right." This person attempts to gain resources—approval, sense of worth, goods, power, money—by accepting and conforming to White social, cultural, and institutional standards, more as an unexamined response to the dominant social mode than an examined explicit pattern of behavior consciously adopted for personal survival. The internal acceptance of these standards as a worldview requires the rejection and devaluation of all that is Black. A Black person who consciously (active acceptance) or unconsciously (passive acceptance) adopts the prevailing White view of the world weakens his or her positive self-concept or positive view of Black people. This consciousness typically causes a Black person to avoid interactions with other Blacks and to desire interactions with Whites, a behavioral pattern that may at first seem to conform to the dominant mode of traditional college campuses or the expectations of some White peers or teachers. Black people in this stage may exhibit these beliefs and behaviors:

Beliefs:
People are people, and if Blacks just work hard they will judged by their merits.
There is no race problem. The problem is with those Blacks who don't want to work and better themselves. They are messing it up for the rest of us.

White people are generally smarter than Black people, and White people
get ahead because they work harder at succeeding than Blacks do.

Behaviors:
Seeks interaction with and validation from Whites and White social
groups and avoids organizations, committees, social groups that focus
on race or racism
Goes along with or excuses racist behavior on the part of Whites.

The transition from acceptance to resistance marks a period that can be
confusing and often painful for both targets (Blacks) and dominants (Whites).
The transition generally evolves over time and usually results from a number
of events that have a cumulative effect. People in an acceptance consciousness begin to be aware of experiences that contradict the acceptance worldview,
experiences they had earlier ignored or passed off as isolated, exceptional
events. Gradually, as a person begins to encounter more dissonant issues,
the isolated incidents form a discernible pattern. The contradictions that
initiate the transition period can arise from interactions with people, social
events, information presented in classes, stories in the media, or responses to
so-called racial incidents on campus. Many students of color as well as White
students were shaken by overt acts of harassment and hostility toward students of color in the late 1980s. Many who had seen racism as a 1960s issue
began to reevaluate their thinking in the light of the numerous acts of disrespect and violence on campus.

Dominant group members experience difficult emotions as they exit
the acceptance stage and enter into the resistance consciousness. These
range from guilt and embarrassment at having been naive or foolish
enough to believe the racist messages they received, to anger and disgust
at the people and institutions that taught them. Emotions seem to be
especially intense for those who were enthusiastic supporters of the
acceptance worldview. As their way of viewing the world crumbles, they
are often afraid and uncertain what the implications of this new awareness will be. Target group members who begin to exit from the stage of
acceptance typically share a reluctant acknowledgment of their collusion
with their own victimization and an emerging understanding of the
harmful effects of holding on to the acceptance consciousness. In Freireian
terms, the members of these target groups begin to become aware of the
many ways they have played host to their oppressor.

Stage Three—Resistance

The initial questioning that begins during the exit phase of acceptance
continues with greater intensity during the third stage, resistance. The
worldview that people adopt at resistance is dramatically different from

that of acceptance. At this stage members of both target and dominant groups begin to understand and recognize racism in many of its complex and multiple manifestations—at the individual and institutional, conscious and unconscious, intentional and unintentional attitudinal, behavioral, and policy levels. Individuals become painfully aware of the numerous ways in which covert as well as overt racism affect them daily as members of racial identity groups.

Resistance Stage for Whites. There are two manifestations of the resistance stage, as there are for the acceptance stage. For Whites in passive resistance there are the beginnings of a critical consciousness of the existence of racism and White people's relationship to it, but it is generally an awareness accompanied by little action or behavioral change. Whites in passive resistance may see the problem but feel personally impotent to affect it. There is a prevailing feeling that the issue is too big and nothing can be done about it, especially by only one concerned person. The active resistance stage is quite different, however. White persons who acquire the active resistance consciousness have a more deeply developed critical consciousness about racism, and also have a sense of personal ownership of the problem. That is, they are aware that they too are racist, and that whatever they do or fail to do is either part of the problem or part of the solution. At this stage, Whites understand that they have internalized racial prejudice, misinformation, and lies about themselves as Whites and about people of color. They also realize that their behavior has been racist in at least a passive sense and perhaps at times in active, conscious ways.

The resistance stage engenders powerful emotions in White persons, ranging from embarrassment and anger to disbelief, shame, guilt, and occasionally despair. Some Whites in active resistance become so distressed at being part of an oppressive dominant group that they distance themselves from other Whites and White culture by gravitating to communities of color and trying to adopt a new identity. This response is particularly common among college-age students who live in a campus environment where exploring new identities, political orientations, and different roles is commonplace. This behavior also reflects the confusion of White students at this stage, who are in a process of rejecting the racism and oppressiveness of White individuals, institutions, and culture and as such do not want to see themselves as part of that group. Another indicator of the learning process is the realization that confronting and changing the White community is the special responsibility of Whites who are antiracist. The focus of energy shifts, from being a good "liberal" to people of color, to being a real agent of change with one's White peers.

At the active resistance stage, White people may hold the following types of attitudes and beliefs:

Racism in the United States is White racism and I have been infected
with it.

The cultures of Black, Latino, Asian, and Native people have been mis-
represented by racism.

Racism is systemic and is not simply prejudice or discrimination in one
facet of life.

Whites in active resistance may show the following behavioral
indicators:

Indiscriminately challenging racism in many spheres, by letter writing,
picketing, and verbal confrontations

Expressing solidarity with people of color through wearing buttons,
participating in marches, donating money, and so on

Distancing themselves from White culture and people, and simultaneously "adopting" or borrowing the traditions and cultural expressions of communities of color.

Whites in passive resistance may have attitudes and beliefs similar to
those of Whites in active resistance, but the behavioral indicators may be
absent. For many Whites in passive resistance, a key indicator of the
stage may be attempts to "drop out."

Resistance Stage for Blacks. The acknowledgment of the existence
of racism and its negative effects is typical of one who is exiting the
acceptance stage. This stage is usually followed by the first manifestation
of the resistance stage—active, often vehement questioning. Once a
Black person has acknowledged the existence of racism, he or she usually
desires to find out more about it. These values, moral codes, and codes of
personal and professional development, handed down by the dominant
White culture and those who collude with their victimization, are the
first things to be scrutinized through the lens of this new consciousness.
Gradually the target group member becomes more skilled at identifying
the existence of racist premises that have been woven into the fabric of
social experience. This person finds that his or her hostility toward
White people, as well as toward fellow Blacks (or other targeted people
of color) who collude with White people, is intensifying.

The often overt expression of hostile reactions to the existence and
effects of racism marks the transition from the entry to the adoption phase
of the resistance stage. It is at this point in the resistance stage that the
Black individual has fully internalized the antithesis of the acceptance
stage of development. It is here that the person fully experiences anger,
pain, and rage. The combination of these emotions with a more intellectual understanding of the manifestations and effects of racism may appear

to be all consuming. Some Black students who enter this stage during their college years may find it difficult to remain focused on course work, especially if that work seems irrelevant to their emerging concern for Blackness and for racial issues. We have seen some students at this stage become heavily involved with student groups and with campus efforts that have an activist focus. Many of these students are motivated, capable, and gifted academically. Their turning away from their course work is not due to inability. Rather they are drawn in a compelling and often consuming way to engage in social action, through seminars, teach-ins, demonstrations, and other efforts to confront racism and effect change on their campus regarding racial issues. In other instances, the Black person may find that to experience the resistance stage fully results in the loss of the "benefits" that were acquired when the acceptance consciousness was adopted. Blacks may choose the path of passive resistance, in the hope that they will be able to stay in favor with White society while rejecting racism. Typically, this strategy proves too frustrating and contradictory to sustain. For most Blacks at this stage the primary task is to discontinue the pattern of collusion with their own victimization. It is time to cleanse their consciousness of those internalized racist notions that have served to stifle or retard their personal development and to stop passively accepting the racism of their environment.

During the course of the resistance stage, the Black person discovers a greater scope for action and a sense of personal power. At this stage, students who rail against the "system" discover that they can make that system respond. While the power that is gained at this stage is not of the same type and quantity available to the dominant group, it is power nonetheless. The student recognizes that to varying degrees and in a variety of situations, he or she can stop things from happening. For many this is the first lesson in personal and social power. Also during the course of the resistance stage, the person begins to recognize that a considerable amount of energy has been put into unlearning as well as undoing considerable earlier programming about his or her identity as a Black person. The primary focus at this stage is the exact reverse of acceptance: it is directed toward being clear about "who I am not." This person is now ready to put energy into the questions "Who am I? Who are we?" Some indicators of the resistance stage for Blacks may include the following attitudes and behaviors:

Challenging and confronting Whites, especially those in positions of authority; and challenging or writing off Black faculty and administrators who are seen as not Black enough or as colluding with the White system

Testing the credentials of Black staff and faculty to determine whether they are truly revolutionary

Denigrating all that is White, and simultaneously glorifying all that is Black, in an unrelenting manner.

Stage 4—Redefinition

The transition from resistance to redefinition occurs when members of both racial groups realize that they do not really know who they are, racially speaking, or what their racial group membership means to them. At resistance, they recognized that their sense of themselves as Whites or as Blacks has been defined for them in a White racist environment, and they actively sought to question it and reject aspects of it. Now they are no longer actively consumed by rejection, but the loss of prior self-definition of Blackness or Whiteness leaves them with a void. Attempts to grapple with the question what it means to be White and antiracist, or what it means to be Black, lead to the redefinition stage.

Redefinition Stage for Whites. Having experienced a period of conflict at the resistance stage, Whites are now beginning to move beyond this conflict toward a resolution and a new racial identity. They begin to refocus or redirect their energy in order to define Whiteness in a way that is not dependent on racism or on the existence of perceived deficiencies in other groups.

Before this stage, Whites are not terribly concerned with their racial identity. Up to this point they have been focusing on people of color as "different from" or deficient or developing a consciousness of racism and reacting to it. The consequences of experiencing the resistance stage has left Whites feeling negative about their Whiteness, confused about their role in dealing with racism, and isolated from much of their racial group. Therefore, developing a deeper understanding of the meaning of Whiteness and its connection to racism, together with those aspects of White, European American culture that affirm their own needs as individual members of that social group, is a necessary part of the redefinition stage for Whites. In contrast to the negative feelings about being White at the earlier Resistance stage, Whites at redefinition can begin to develop a new sense of comfort and identification with their cultural heritage. This recognition of the strengths of White culture and people results in a feeling of pride in the group membership, without a personal feeling of superiority, and without disclaiming the larger system of societal dominance focused on at the earlier resistance stage. There is a recognition that all cultures and racial groups have unique and different traits that enrich the human experience, and that no race or culture is superior to another. They are all unique, different, and adaptive.

Redefinition Stage for Blacks. The redefinition stage is the point in the developmental process at which the Black person is concerned with defining himself or herself in terms that are independent of the perceived strengths or weaknesses of Whites and the dominant White culture. The redefinition stage is particularly significant because it is here that Black people shift their attention and energy away from a concern for the nature of their interaction with dominants toward a concern for primary contact and interaction with other Blacks at the same stage of conscious-ness. Unlike the Black person at the acceptance and resistance stages, the Black person with a redefinition consciousness is not concerned either with emulating or rejecting dominants and dominant culture. The rede-fining person does not see interaction with dominants as necessary and useful in the quest for a positive or nurturing sense of self and racial identity. Because renaming is the primary concern in this person's life, he or she begins a search for paradigms that will facilitate the accomplish-ment of this task.

This search can begin in a number of places, but for most Black people it seems to begin with the conscious or unconscious formation of a new reference group. As mentioned above, it is critical that this new reference group consist of other Blacks with a redefinition perspective. Black people at this stage are particularly concerned with the perspective of other Black people and as a consequence tend to limit their interac-tions to Blacks, where this is an option. But this type of behavior is often viewed negatively by members of both dominant and target groups at earlier stages of consciousness. Whereas students in the resistance stage who are members of targeted groups are generally labeled troublemak-ers, students in redefinition may be labeled separatist or self-segregating. Black students at this stage have a particular need to participate in, or create where none exist, programs, centers, or housing units where they can interact closely and maintain dialogue with other Black students in the same stage. While some Black students in redefinition may begin to see connections between the racism that Blacks experience and the racism experienced by other people of color (Native Americans, Hispan-ics, and Asian Americans), they may not be invested in forming alliances or coalitions with members of those groups. The psychological tasks at this stage are very in-group (that is, Black) centered, and adopting a multicultural worldview, rather than a Black worldview, may be prema-ture at this point.

It may be difficult for non-Blacks to interact with Blacks who are occupied with redefinition issues. Non-Blacks may fail to understand that the redefinition stage is chiefly concerned with engaging in relation-ships and activities that will further the search for new and different ways of redefining one's self and one's social group membership. Old alle-giances are being reevaluated. Thus many relationships that appeared essential in the past seem not to be as important at this stage.

The search for a new understanding of Blackness often begins by reclaiming the group heritage. Revisiting or uncovering their heritage or culture, Blacks often find values, traditions, customs, philosophical as-sumptions, and concepts of time, work, and family that are appealing and nurturing. They find that many elements of Black culture that have been handed down through the generations still affect their lives, and the uniqueness of their group becomes clearer. They come to understand that they are more than the victims of racism, more than just people who are not the same as the dominant group. These targets come to experience their Blackness in a way that engenders pride.

Indicators of the redefinition stage for Blacks include:

Literally changing their names, taking on African or Muslim names
Demonstrating a concern for presenting a Black perspective or an African or Afrocentric perspective in a variety of settings
Changing friendships, academic major, career directions, or choice of living situation and redirecting energy and focus from White-oriented choices to Black people and Black-oriented concerns.

The redefinition stage is seen less often in the traditional college-age White student than in the Black college student. In fact, although more students of color may enter this stage during college, their numbers are not large. It is more likely that both White students and Black students will enter college at the (passive) acceptance stage and experience primarily the (active or passive) resistance stages only during their college years. For this reason we have chosen to provide more detail about these earlier two stages and have restricted our description of redefinition and internalization to the basics.

Stage 5—Internalization

The transition from the redefinition stage to the internalization stage occurs when an individual begins to integrate some of the newly defined values, beliefs, and behaviors into all aspects of life. As with any other developmental task, it takes time and a variety of opportunities for the new aspects of a person's identity to begin the process of integration with the rest of that person's identity. When the redefined sense of racial identity is fully integrated, the new values or beliefs occur naturally and are internalized as a part of the person.

Indicators of internalization for Blacks include:

Recognition that their Black identity is a critical part of them, but not the only significant aspect of their identity
Ability to consider other identity issues, and other issues of oppression, since some resolution of the struggle for a redefined Black identity has occurred
Ability to work effectively with Blacks at all stages of identity development in assisting them to deal with whatever issues their stage of development presents, and not judge or act punitively toward Blacks

who are at earlier stages, but help them achieve a positive Black identity.

Indicators of internalization for Whites include:

A clear sense of their own self-interests as members of the White group in ending racism; acting on that self-interest to confront racial oppression proactively

An understanding of the uniqueness of their cultural backgrounds; not seeing others as "culturally different" and Whites as "normal," but rather understanding how White European American culture is different as well.

Applications and Conclusions

It perhaps is self-evident at this point in our discussion that college campuses are frequently the arena in which the processes of developing the racial identity of students, faculty, and staff are visibly played out. One has to look no further than White student unions and acts of racial harassment to see Whites in active acceptance. One can also see the stage of active resistance and occasionally redefinition appearing in the "Third World Affairs" pages of student newspapers and in race-specific cultural and social centers, such as Malcolm X centers, Latino student caucuses, and American Indian student centers. It should also be clear that our campuses are places where students and others interact with each other from their respective, frequently clashing stages of racial identity development. How should faculty and administrators respond?

1. *It should be our goal as educators to facilitate development in students, not stifle it or hide from it.* As difficult as it is to do, we believe that it is necessary first to acknowledge and accept wherever a student is in his or her developmental journey, not to condemn or try to hasten it. Only if we understand and respond to each student's developmental stage can we expect that student to grow at his or her own pace.

It is not easy for faculty and administrators to absorb students' anger as expressed at the resistance stage. Well-intentioned administrators are particularly vulnerable to onslaughts from students who are (rightfully) angered by acts of racism or harassment on campus. We have seen administrators disregard students' anger or call for an investigation or a policy change, dismissing the behavior as mere adolescent "acting out" or, more cynically, as the "annual Spring protest." As difficult as it may be, administrators, especially those who are White, do represent a power structure that students must confront: first, because most institutions frankly deserve to be challenged, since no campus is free of racism; second, because students need to exercise their emerging sense of empowerment, as full citizens; third, because their often newly established perspective, within resistance, focuses their attention on resistance as a total and absorbing worldview. We have also seen errors in misinterpreting White students' assaults against students of color as "pranks" or late adolescent acting out rather than expressions of a worldview of active acceptance of White supremacy. We describe active acceptance as a "stage," but our experience is that not all students will move beyond it, and students should not be allowed to violate other students' rights because "it is just a stage they are going through."

2. *As faculty and staff, we should look at these stages in the light of our own life experiences.* Where are we in our own racial identity development process? None of us are neutral players in this world; we bring all our "baggage" to our profession. Our racial identity development stage influences the curriculum we develop, our choice of bibliography, and even how we organize our classroom environments. For example, we know of a recent situation where a White professor, acting out of "liberal" beliefs, refused to begin a class until the Black students dispersed themselves around the classroom, and stopped "segregating" themselves.

3. *We should not be surprised by the ways in which our students interact.* "Vertical" social group relationships (dominant and targeted) and "horizontal" relationships (within or across targeted groups) (Jackson and Hardiman, 1988) can express themselves in sharp differences of ideology or belief, which can seem confusing if one looks for monolithic ethnic and cultural expressions without considering the role of individual racial identity filters as well.

4. *We should understand broad differences in social identity perspective.* Recognizing that social identity is the generic of which racial identity is a particular instance (Jackson and Hardiman, 1988; Jones, 1990) will enable college teachers and administrators to prepare for differences of understanding and belief by students across their range of social group differences as filtered through their individual developmental lenses. For example, Black male students may be at one perspective in their racial identity (active resistance, perhaps, or redefinition), but at another concerning sexism or anti-Semitism (passive or active acceptance possibly); similarly, Jewish female students may be in active resistance or redefinition with regard to their Jewish identity and at another place on racism or heterosexism. The same unevenness among racial, ethnic, and other social identity profiles is just as likely to characterize faculty and administrators as students.

In this chapter we have presented a model of racial identity development for Black and White Americans and discussed the application of racial identity development stages as filters for understanding the divergent and often conflicting behavior of students on campus as they grapple with racial issues. We also argued at the beginning of this chapter for the consideration of issues of dominance and oppression in our discussions of diversity issues in higher education, because we see social group differences and their accompanying forms of group bias and discrimination as inseparable.

We have suggested in this chapter that faculty and administrators' failure to understand and respect the development of racial identity in their students can lead to inappropriate and ineffective responses to volatile racial situations on campus. We present this model to inform behavior and the selection of strategies and responses, but we caution against anyone's using this model simplistically to label or stereotype or pigeonhole students or others. We present the stages for purposes of initial understanding, as if a person were to move neatly in totality from one stage to the next, whereas the reality is that most people are in several stages simultaneously, holding simultaneously different perspectives on the complex range of issues and questions that enter into their equally complicated racial identity. Rather than misusing it as a set of labels or new stereotypes, our hope is that readers will use this model to understand better the racial identity component of their own developmental processes, identify the individual characteristics or cues that constitute the broad brush strokes called "developmental stages," and thereby understand and respect the racial identity developmental processes that are likely to be stimulated by rapid changes in our social world and refracted back even more intensely onto our college campuses.

References

Abrams, D., and Hogg, M. A. (eds.). *Social Identity Theory: Constructive and Critical Advances.* New York: Springer-Verlag, 1990.

Border, L.L.B., and Chism, N.V.N. (eds.). *Teaching for Diversity.* New Directions for Teaching and Learning, no. 49. San Francisco: Jossey-Bass, 1992.

Cross, W. E., Jr. "The Negro-to-Black Conversion Experience: Toward a Psychology of Black Liberation." *Black World,* 1971, *20* (9), 13–27.

Cross, W. E., Jr. "Models of Psychological Nigrescence: A Literature Review." *Journal of Black Psychology,* 1978, *5* (1), 13–31.

Cross, W. E., Jr. *Shades of Black: Diversity in African-American Identity.* Philadelphia: Temple University Press, 1991.

Cross, W. E., Jr., Parham, T. A., and Helms, J. E. "Nigrescence Revisited: Theory and Research." In R. L. Jones (ed.), *Advances in Black Psychology.* Vol. 1. Berkeley, Calif.: Cobb & Henry, in press.

Dalton, J. C. (ed.). *Racism on Campus: Confronting Racial Bias Through Peer Interventions.* New Directions for Student Services, no. 56. San Francisco: Jossey-Bass, 1991.

Derman-Sparks, L., Higa, C. T., and Sparks, B. "Children, Race and Racism: How Race Awareness Develops." *Interracial Books for Children Bulletin,* 1980, *11* (3, 4), 3–9.

Hardiman, R. "White Identity Development Theory." Unpublished manuscript, University of Massachusetts, Amherst, 1979.

Hardiman, R. "White Identity Development: A Process-Oriented Model for Describing the Racial Consciousness of White Americans." Unpublished doctoral dissertation, University of Massachusetts, Amherst, 1982.

Hayes-Bautista, D. E. "Becoming Chicano: A 'Dis-Assimilation' Theory of Transformation of Ethnic Identity." Unpublished doctoral dissertation, University of California, San Francisco, 1974.

Helms, J. E. *Black and White Racial Identity: Theory, Research and Practice.* Westport, Conn.: Greenwood Press, 1990.

Ho, M. K. *Family Therapy with Ethnic Minorities.* Newbury Park, Calif.: Sage, 1987.

Jackson, B. W. "Black Identity Development." In L. Golubschick and B. Persky (eds.), *Urban Social and Educational Issues.* Dubuque, Iowa: Kendall/Hunt, 1976a.

Jackson, B. W. "The Function of a Theory of Black Identity Development in Achieving Relevance in Education for Black Students." Unpublished doctoral dissertation, University of Massachusetts, Amherst, 1976b.

Jackson, B. W., and Hardiman, R. "Oppression: Conceptual and Developmental Analysis." In M. Adams and L. S. Marchesani (eds.), *Racial and Cultural Diversity, Curricular Content, and Classroom Dynamics: A Manual for College Teachers.* Amherst: University of Massachusetts, 1988.

Jones, W. T. "Perspectives on Ethnicity." In L. V. Moore (ed.), *Evolving Theoretical Perspectives on Students.* New Directions for Student Services, no. 51. San Francisco: Jossey-Bass, 1990.

Kim, J. "Processes of Asian American Identity Development: A Study of Japanese American Women's Perceptions of Their Struggle to Achieve Positive Identities as Americans of Asian Ancestry." Unpublished doctoral dissertation, University of Massachusetts, Amherst, 1981.

Levine, A. "Editorial: The Meaning of Diversity." *Change,* 1991, 23 (5), 4–5.

Mann, B. A., and Moser, R. M. "A Model for Designing Peer-Initiated Activities to Promote Racial Awareness and an Appreciation of Differences." In J. Dalton (ed.), *Racism on Campus: Confronting Racial Bias Through Peer Interventions.* New Directions for Student Services, no. 56. San Francisco: Jossey-Bass, 1991.

Smith, E. J. "Ethnic Identity Development: Toward the Development of a Theory Within the Context of Majority/Minority Status." *Journal of Counseling & Development,* 1991, 70 (1), 181–188.

Tatum, B. D. "Talking About Race, Learning About Racism: The Application of Racial Identity Development Theory in the Classroom." *Harvard Educational Review,* 1992, 62 (1), 1–24.

Wijeyesinghe, C. "Towards An Understanding of the Racial Identity of Bi-Racial People: The Experience of Racial Self-Identification of African-American Euro-American Adults and the Factors Affecting Their Choices of Racial Identity." Unpublished doctoral dissertation, University of Massachusetts, Amherst, 1992.

RITA HARDIMAN is on the faculty of the Social Justice Education Program, School of Education, University of Massachusetts, Amherst. She is also a partner in New Perspectives, Inc., a firm that specializes in providing training and consultation services related to social diversity and social justice in organizational settings.

BAILEY W. JACKSON is founding faculty member of the Social Justice Education Program, School of Education, and currently dean of the School of Education, University of Massachusetts, Amherst.

Handling intergroup bias issues in the classroom may stimulate instructor anxiety but also provides opportunities for self-understanding. This chapter describes some of the common anxieties and offers ways of coping.

Bias Issues in the Classroom: Encounters with the Teaching Self

Gerald Weinstein, Kathy Obear

> To bring these cultures into the classroom is to confront the ignominious as well as the glorious side of our history. Some faculty fear they will be unable to handle the inevitable conflict, anger, frustration, and confusion of their students, as well as their own fear, anger, or feelings of guilt. "I am not prepared to be a social worker," they cry: "I am a scholar and teacher!" This fear is very real and is, in fact, symptomatic of the profound challenge educators face in our times. It is the "self" that is really at stake here, the very notion of "personal identity" around which liberal education has evolved.
> —Wilkerson, 1992, p. 59

It is a rare instructor who would claim that raising issues of racism, sexism, or similar intergroup bias issues in a class is a neutral activity. Because the content of intergroup issues is so cognitively complex and emotionally charged, it very often challenges not only the students but also the instructor at many personal levels. We contend that an instructor's ability and willingness to anticipate and monitor her or his intrapersonal dynamics about this teaching situation is a necessary component of classroom preparation.

Expectations are increasing for faculty not only to be sensitive to issues of gender, race, ethnicity, and multiculturalism, regardless of their academic specialization, but also to treat these issues as part of their teaching responsibilities. Our own experience has been to conduct workshops and courses whose express content is bias reduction, a primary objective of which is to increase learner awareness of intergroup difference and injustice and to enhance intergroup attitudes and behaviors. Even though the reader may not identify with such a direct approach, we hope that our experience and our work on classroom dynamics with graduate teaching assistants and faculty colleagues will prove helpful to those who find themselves, planfully or serendipitously, confronted by the need to deal with these issues in their classroom.

Few college teachers have been trained to manage or treat bias in the classroom. When they first begin to weave these issues into their courses, as a matter of personal choice or as the result of questions stemming from greater student diversity, they may experience something similar to what in the international cross-cultural situation is known as culture shock. When we are in a familiar instructional setting, students usually respond to us in relatively predictable ways. Our sense of ourselves as teachers and persons is maintained. However, as Zaharna (1989) argues, when "sojourners" enter a new, unfamiliar culture they often find that their usual behaviors meet with atypical responses. The result is culture shock. If we consider the intergroup antibias instructional setting as a form of cross-cultural experience, then what Zaharna, addressing cross-cultural training, labeled *self-shock* is applicable here. Culture shock stimulates self-doubt and confusion and results in self-shock, which is essentially a challenge to one's core self-image. The more representative the instructor is of the socially privileged members of our society, the more probable that he or she will feel like a sojourner in this teaching situation.

Applied to the antibias instructional setting, atypical interactions challenge our self-image as competent, clear-thinking professionals. Zaharna points out that since our identities are products of social interaction, the more intense the interaction, the more our identities are confronted. We are responding to a social form of physical stress, so that instead of trying to save our skins we are attempting to save face—that is, to save our identities as knowledgeable, detached, and professorial. It is this challenge to identity that seems to be the basis for the constellation of fears described in the following discussion.

In this chapter we would like to differentiate some of the intrapersonal emotional dimensions that we and some of our colleagues have examined when involved in antibias teaching. We do this in order to explore the extent to which our personal experience may be useful to colleagues and to illustrate that this form of teaching has a critical personal component that is rarely described in pedagogical writings. If this personal component can be clarified we may be able to recognize certain aspects of an instructor's intrapersonal dynamics as common, expected, and shared— in other words, normal. We would hope that such recognition might lead to greater faculty willingness to assume the risks involved in treating bias issues as part of the pedagogical repertoire. In addition, understanding and monitoring our own responses seems essential to how well we, as instructors, are able to facilitate the emotional dynamics of the group. We need to know what our emotional boundaries and hot spots are in order to understand how they may constrain or enhance our approach to instruction.

Antibias instruction stimulates a wide range of emotions, and the most common, in the instructor and the student, is fear. The major reservoirs of fear reside in the instructor, the participants, and the social issue being confronted. Both we and our students bring multilayered sets of fears coupled with self-protective behaviors to particular intergroup issues the very existence of which depends on fears. Each particular issue such as racism or sexism has its own unique configuration of fear components. It is the contents of these reservoirs that require coordination, mediation, and channeling by the antibias instructor.

Recently, we asked a group of twenty-five university faculty colleagues from different disciplines, who had gathered to discuss the handling of racism issues in their undergraduate classes, to respond anonymously on paper to the question "What makes you nervous about raising issues of racism in your classroom?" Their responses plus responses to similar questions raised by others (Katz, 1983; Janha, 1988; Noonan, 1988; Cones, Janha, and Noonan, 1983) confirmed our sense of the linkage between our antibias teaching experience and theirs. We have grouped some of the most commonly shared fears under the following headings:

1. Confronting my own social and cultural identity conflicts:
   Having to become more aware of my own attitudes regarding my
      group memberships and identifications
   Feeling guilty, ashamed, or embarrassed for behaviors and attitudes
      of members of my own group.
2. Having to confront or being confronted with my own bias:
   Being labeled racist, sexist, and so on
   Finding prejudice within myself
   Romanticizing the targeted group
   Having to question my own assumptions
   Having to be corrected by members of the targeted group
   Having to face my own fears of the targeted group.
3. Responding to biased comments:
   Responding to biased comments from the targeted group
   Hearing biased comments from dominant members while targeted
      members are present
   Responding to biased remarks from members of my own social
      group.
4. Doubts and ambivalence about my own competency:
   Having to expose my own struggles with the issue
   Not knowing the latest "politically correct" language

Feeling uncertain about what I am saying
Feeling that I will never unravel the complexities of the issue
Being told by a student that I don't know what I'm talking about
Making a mistake.
5. Need for learner approval:
Making students frustrated, frightened, or angry
Leaving my students shaken and confused and not being able to fix it.
6. Handling intense emotions; losing control:
Not knowing how to respond to angry comments
Having discussion blow up
Having anger directed at me
Being overwhelmed by strong emotions engendered by the discussion
Feeling strong emotions being stimulated in myself.

For the remainder of this chapter we will elaborate some of these fears and offer suggestions that we and our colleagues have found useful in our attempts to cope with them. However, before we do, we would like to remind the reader that techniques cannot be applied to all teaching situations in some formulaic way that avoids discomfort. Raising bias issues in the classroom in our opinion can be stimulating, but never comfortable, especially when group interaction is part of the process. In addition, although we treat these issues as if they were separate or discrete, they do, in fact, overlap and constantly interact.

Let me begin by using myself as an example. (The first-person perspective that follows reflects the personal experience of the first author in the hope that it provides an example of self-monitoring and encourages reader identification.)

1. and 2. *My own social identities and biases.* Even though I come into the classroom as a professional teacher, I do not leave my social identities at the door. I am a blend of such identities, for example, white, male, Jewish, heterosexual, beyond middle age, working-class background, now middle class. Especially when I am conducting Jewish oppression workshops, I am constantly reminded of my conflicts about being at the same time a targeted subordinate group member and a dominant group member with all of the inequities and privileges associated with each.

Toward each oppressed group affected by personal and institutional bias in our society I have certain inherent shortcomings in awareness. That is, built into my privileges as a white male, I have certain areas of limited vision. In spite of a lifelong attempt to diminish those limitations, I still need to monitor the gaps in my knowledge and sensitivity, areas in which I still have ignorance, fear, and uncertainty regarding the issue. I need to know what issues or facets of issues I tend to avoid and whether that avoidance is a constructive choice or merely a rationalization. The fears that drive my avoidance are of finding out how homophobic, racist, or sexist I still am, which would conflict with my ideal image of myself as an aware person engaged in helping others with their awareness. Moreover, some aspects of my racism or sexism or homophobia are difficult to recognize and root out.

In addition, I can be at different phases or stages of gender or racial identity awareness on different issues (see Chapter Two), for example, at a beginning phase with respect to sexism, where I may still accept parts of the status quo, and at a more advanced phase with respect to racism, where I actively attempt to interrupt racist behavior in my sphere of influence. Two potential errors can occur. The first is to believe that sophistication about one issue automatically transfers to others; the second, that I can totally erase all racist, sexist, homophobic, and other fears of difference in myself in time to teach my class.

Ideally, people who have been victimized by bigotry should be highly sensitive and vigilant when groups other than their own are also victims. Unfortunately, experiencing bias does not automatically render one an expert or liberate one from bias toward another group. I have been exposed to Jewish racism and sexism, African American anti-Semitism and sexism, and antisexists who are racist and anti-Semitic. I always harbor the wish that all targeted group members would be allies and partners in interrupting bias in all of its forms. However, wishing does not make it so. When I am confronted with bias toward my group from other targeted members, African Americans, or women, I have to surmount my fear of alienating those whom I thought were "on my side" and challenge their beliefs in the same way that I would anyone else. However, in the process it is important that I provide continuous evidence to such members that I am sensitive to their targeted group issues.

As a targeted group member, especially when I am teaching about that group's issues, I am also vulnerable to all the dominant group signals concerning my group. Some version of all the stereotypical statements and attitudes that have pursued me my entire life are bound to be expressed. I always experience those expressions and attitudes with some degree of pain, for they restimulate past fears and responses to oppressive behaviors toward both me personally and my group as a whole. When I hear those expressions I may get angry and want to retaliate, but I know that acting directly on my feelings may be inappropriate and counterproductive to the goals of the session and my role as teacher and facilitator. By anticipating a range of typical responses that I have experienced before and encouraging them in structured ways, I can prepare myself to use these triggers intentionally and constructively during the session.

3. *Responding to biased expressions.* Targeted group members usually have a long history of developing sensitivity to certain negative cues. They have been subjected to them, suffered from them, discussed and

thought about them throughout the course of their lives. Therefore, most are very sensitive to such signals. Typically, members of nontargeted groups have been so effectively and monoculturally socialized that they consider their languaging "natural." They are usually unaware of whom they are cueing and are shocked when someone takes offense. We call these cues and signals *triggers*.

Triggers are recurring phenomena in our workshops and classes. There are certain words, phrases, or concepts usually communicated by members of the nontargeted group about a targeted group or individual that signal an oppressive attitude toward that group. Some are blatantly obvious: "a woman's place is in the home"; "Blacks seem to want to stick together"; "the Jewish media"; "homosexuals are abnormal." Others are more subtle: "I don't see race as the issue, we're all human beings, it's a matter of love"; "I don't see people as black, brown, red, yellow, or white. To me they're just people"; "I always hear Jews making fun of themselves"; "they aren't the only ones who suffered"; "they're just not as qualified."

Triggers may immediately stimulate the defenses of the person whose group is being commented on, or an ally of that group, and can elicit intense emotional reactions. Responses to triggers can be especially volatile in a mixed setting of targeted and nontargeted groups. What often occurs is that one person makes the statement that triggers another student to respond in a confrontational or defensive style. The original "trigger giver" often will argue for the truth of what was said, or state that it was never his or her intention to give offense and that the respondent seems to be "overly sensitive." This comment in turn may become another trigger. The exchange typically continues with a painful and unproductive debate of increasing intensity. It can sometimes lead to the shutdown of group discussion in stifling silence and barely controlled frustration. It is a fearful situation for the instructor, and one that is very difficult to manage.

An alternative is to raise the general issue of triggers at the outset and describe what they are and how they are experienced differently by members of the dominant and targeted groups.

It is important to handle the discussion of triggers so that members of both dominant and targeted groups are validated as individuals. Targeted members have a right to ask that others be sensitive to their own language. Trigger givers need to understand that they came by their socialization innocently. They did not ask to be raised in racist, sexist, classist, homophobic, anti-Semitic society. They do not need to be assisted in castigating themselves but encouraged to learn how they have been socialized and how to gain control over their thoughts and feelings. One measure of success may be the extent to which individuals can self-monitor potential triggers for different groups.

A principle that will undergird many of my suggestions is to plan for anticipated responses in part by establishing ground rules. That principle is demonstrated by initially introducing the concept of triggers and having learners supply their own examples before any arise spontaneously. A useful ground rule might be: "Anytime someone feels triggered, including myself, we can say 'trigger' or 'there is one for me' and we post the trigger on newsprint. Later in our session we can review them." By not having to deal with the trigger at that moment we create some distance between the person who gave the trigger and analysis of the trigger itself. The focus can then be on understanding the concept rather than dealing with the defenses of individuals. (For a more extensive description of ground rules appropriate for this situation, see Cannon, 1990.)

4. *My own competency and ambivalence.* As college faculty members we are paid to communicate something about which we are assumed to have expertise. Learners view the teacher from a variety of perspectives: as a font of knowledge, someone who "knows the answers," or perhaps as someone who helps them think about ideas. To the degree that we need to appear certain of what we know, we may find it difficult to encounter hot spots or knowledge gaps exposed by our interactions with the students. This is especially true when targeted group members other than my own describe perspectives to which I am not yet sensitive. Unless I can admit to the students that I am still in the process of learning and unlearning and that there are areas about which I still need to be educated, I may give the impression that there are simple solutions to which I have access. This attitude places great pressure on us as instructors to have "the answer." One way of diminishing this pressure is to disclose our uncertainties to the students. "When instructors voice ambivalence, they acknowledge the legitimacy of that powerful emotion, and make it possible for students to acknowledge theirs" (Noonan, 1988, pp. 82–83). It also models that unlearning prejudice is a lifelong process and another way of demonstrating expertise.

5. *Need for learner approval.* "Learners will take out their frustrations on the trainers. . . . They will resist certain learning activities. . . . [Experienced] trainers will recognize that as the program progresses toward its more provocative segments, the trainer may become less rather than more popular with the learners, and they will accept that being liked is not always synonymous with being effective as a trainer" (Paige, 1986, pp. 139–140).

Whenever I consider what it is I would accept as evidence of a successful class, I usually fantasize students with smiling faces and high scores on my student evaluations. Students would uniformly say, "Great class, I really got a lot out of it. I'm really excited by what I learned." That is, most of the feedback would be positive. What makes antibias teaching difficult for me is that although students will often leave having been visibly moved and stimulated, others leave feeling frustrated, upset, and confused. I used to regard the latter situation as evidence of my failure as an instructor. It was not until we ran a racism workshop for a community college in which the entire administration and faculty were involved that my concept of what constituted successful teaching began to change. On finishing the weekend-long session, the participants were not smiling. They soberly reported that they were confused, worried, and upset about all that been experienced and discussed. On the way home my co-leader and I felt that the workshop had been a failure. Over the next three to five years, however, we kept getting reports of systematic changes in that institution that promoted greater racial equity and awareness and that were directly attributed to the workshop.

Confronting bias issues should involve anxiety, confusion, anger, and sadness as well as positive stimulation. It is important to remind ourselves that as much as we crave the learners' approval, a sense of well-being and long-term learning are not necessarily synonymous. It may be necessary intentionally to create a tension between the participants' deeply rooted beliefs and a variety of alternative perspectives. A better indicator of the effectiveness of antibias education might be to have participants leave (1) with more questions than when they came in, (2) wanting to know more, and (3) questioning the core assumptions of their own socialization.

6. *Dealing with emotional intensity; losing control.* A friend once told me that if she were to inscribe a motto on her family's coat of arms it would read: "Thou shalt not make a scene." Any indications of conflict or negativity in her family would have to be inferred by an observer. That type of socialization might lead such a person in her instructor role to avoid, deny, or ignore some of the important and necessary emotional dynamics taking place in the group. It is not surprising that how we were socialized to encounter emotions affects how we will deal with the emotional conflicts that inevitably arise when dealing with intergroup bias in our professional role. On the one hand, I may be distrustful of people who express themselves in ways that seem incongruent with what they are feeling. On the other hand, I may be impressed by those who seem to be able to glide through the most difficult discourse with an air of controlled calm.

Some instructors were taught and believe that emotions have no place in academe and design their instruction to control or minimize emotional expressions. Angry students may be viewed as "volatile" or "aggressive"; crying students as "weak," "emotionally unstable," or "damaged" by an interaction. As a result, instructors may distance themselves from many of the core issues and conflicts that are central to antibias education and end by merely skimming the surface.

Regardless of one's past exposure, dealing with tension, anger, and conflict in the classroom is always difficult. Many of us as college teachers are not comfortable conducting a course in which all feelings are encouraged to be expressed and become course content, such as in T-groups or encounter-type groups. However, completely ignoring feelings that are stimulated by this content denies the salience and the significance of the issue and keeps important aspects unexplored. So I try to seek a balance between feeling expression and reasoned discourse. I do it by building into the design structured ways for emotions to be explored intrapersonally and then shared with others. These structures allow me to explore territory I would otherwise avoid in class (for examples, see Weinstein, 1988). I would rather anticipate and deliberately plan for affective expression, knowing of course that the unexpected can and does occur.

If we were left to follow our natural inclinations, many of us would do everything possible to avoid conflict in our classrooms. My own background has contributed to this equation: you are unsafe when you are in conflict; therefore in order to be safe, avoid conflict. I know, however, that the most significant learning may result from what is referred to in cognitive development literature as a "knowledge disturbance" or a disequilibrium (Keil, 1984), and that these disturbances produce conflict essential to human growth and development (Benne, 1982; Miller, 1976). It is useful to be able to remind myself that certain conflict-generating ideas and activities are essential to my teaching self.

By posing contradictions, pointing out various viewpoints, and introducing new information and concepts, I utilize conflict for learning. Instructors may consider voicing their own ambivalence about stirring up feelings as another preventive action. As Noonan observes, "unacknowledged, the conflict between not wanting to upset others and wanting to pursue truth can silence students and faculty" (1988, p. 83).

Our socialization has taught us how important it is to be in control. Our worst fantasy is that the whole situation will go up in flames. There have been a number of times during my antibias teaching when I have felt totally helpless in dealing with certain interactions. A participant may say something that stimulates great tension and anxiety, and a dense silence overtakes the group. The instructor becomes upset and somewhat paralyzed. All eyes are upon us, waiting to see what we will do, expecting us to take care of the situation. I cannot think of any helpful intervention. We are too upset to think clearly. Its a fearsome moment, one that we may anticipate with dread.

The idea of losing control stimulates what Ellis (1984) calls "catastrophic thinking," that is, the belief that if the thing we fear were ever to happen it would be a grand catastrophe. The idea of losing control blends in with other irrational beliefs, such as that I must always know what I am doing, or I am not professionally competent; or that whatever I do must come out right or else I am a failure.

We do not want to look forward to losing control, or expect to feel positively stimulated if we do. Rather, we should regret that it happens sometimes but accept that it is all right. If I were able to be more rational about it I might see that losing control can be a constructive event, one from which I and my students might learn. In fact, students often make fundamental shifts in their perspectives after they have experienced someone's losing control, someone who may have let go enough to share deeper feelings, fears, and experiences.

Raimy (1975) pointed out that fears may comprise a cluster of misconceptions about (1) the harmfulness of the feared situation or object, (2) the probability that one will collapse or disintegrate in the face of the feared situation, and (3) one's fear reaction to the situation as unchangeable. To the extent that I can continually reappraise these interpretations I have the power to diminish the tyrannical qualities of these fears and experience the positively moving aspects of this kind of teaching.

Over the years I have accumulated a few emergency procedures that help me survive these moments.

1. Give participants and myself a brief time out
2. Have people record their own immediate responses in their notebooks or journals
3. Allow each participant to share responses with one other person
4. Ask for any suggestions or ideas from the group.

The purpose of these actions is to get me out of the leadership role temporarily so that I can collect my thoughts. They also change the focus from public to private. Usually, once I gain some distance from the situation I can think clearly and figure out what to do next.

A general approach to helping myself through all the fear issues is mentally to rehearse some cognitive reappraisals of the fearful situations. Self-talk, or self-dialogue, is a way to reappraise. Whenever I used the phrase "I try to remind myself that . . ." I am using self-talk. Here are some useful phrasings I practice:

For insensitive or bigoted remarks: "That person came by their bigotry innocently. What do they fear?"
For anger: "What hurt is that person expressing?"
My own competence: "I don't have to know everything to be an effective teacher. I'm doing the best I can at this time."
Having my own ignorance pinpointed: "I'm still learning."
Conflict and tension: "This is a potential learning opportunity."
Negative feedback: "Everyone doesn't have to approve of me at all times."

My own bigotry: "I know I have bigoted feelings. However, I can acknowledge them and not act on them"; or "I am modeling how unlearning is a lifelong process."

After having surveyed the literature on cross-cultural training, Paige summarizes the personal attributes of the effective cross-cultural trainer (1986, p. 151). These can easily be generalized to any teaching role and especially to one in which bias issues are emphasized. They seem to put a positive frame around many of the self-encounters we have described.

1. Tolerance of ambiguity
2. Cognitive and behavioral flexibility
3. Personal self-awareness, strong personal identity
4. Cultural self-awareness
5. Patience
6. Enthusiasm and commitment
7. Interpersonal sensitivity, relations
8. Tolerance of differences
9. Openness to new experience, peoples
10. Empathy
11. Sense of humility
12. Sense of humor.

We find these items comforting. First, they serve as a kind of checklist of goals directing our own professional development. Second, we find it reassuring that there are generic accessible attributes being identified in related disciplines. It takes some of the mystique out of this complex arena of interpersonal dynamics and helps make some of the solitary and private intrapersonal discourse more public and collaborative.

References

Benne, K. "The Significance of Human Conflict." In L. Porter and B. Mohr (eds.), *Reading Book for Human Relations Training.* Arlington, Va.: National Training Laboratories Institute, 1982.

Cannon, L. W. "Fostering Positive Race, Class, and Gender Dynamics in the Classroom." *Women's Studies Quarterly,* 1990, *18* (1, 2), 126–134.

Cones, J. H., Janha, D., and Noonan, J. F. "Exploring Racial Assumptions with Faculty." In J. H. Cones, J. F. Noonan, and D. Janha (eds.), *Teaching Minority Students.* New Directions for Teaching and Learning, no. 16. San Francisco: Jossey-Bass, 1983.

Ellis, A. "Rational-Emotive Therapy." In R. J. Corsini (ed.), *Current Psychotherapies.* Itasca, Ill.: Peacock, 1984.

Janha, D. "A Report on a Workshop Design to Help Faculty Explore Their Race-Related Assumptions and Practices." In M. Adams and L. Marchesani (eds.), *Racial and Cultural Diversity, Curricular Content, and Classroom Dynamics: A Manual for College Teachers.* Amherst: University of Massachusetts, 1988.

Katz, J. "White Faculty Struggling with the Effects of Racism." In J. H. Cones, J. F. Noonan, and D. Janha (eds.), *Teaching Minority Students*. New Directions in Teaching and Learning, no. 16. San Francisco: Jossey-Bass, 1983.

Keil, F. C. "Mechanisms of Cognitive Development and the Structure of Knowledge." In R. J. Sternberg (ed.), *Mechanisms of Cognitive Development*. New York: W. H. Freeman, 1984.

Miller, J. B. *Toward a New Psychology of Women*. Boston: Beacon Press, 1976.

Noonan, J. F. "Discussing Racial Topics in Class." In M. Adams and L. Marchesani (eds.), *Racial and Cultural Diversity, Curricular Content, and Classroom Dynamics: A Manual for College Teachers*. Amherst: University of Massachusetts, 1988.

Paige, R. M. "Trainer Competencies: The Missing Conceptual Link in Orientation." *International Journal of Intercultural Relations*, 1986, *10* (2), 135–158.

Raimy, V. *Misunderstandings of the Self: Cognitive Psychotherapy and the Misconception Hypothesis.* San Francisco: Jossey-Bass, 1975.

Weinstein, G. "Design Elements for Intergroup Awareness Training." *Journal for Specialists in Group Work,* 1988, *13* (2), 96–103.

Wilkerson, M. B. "Beyond the Graveyard: Engaging Faculty Involvement." *Change,* 1992, *24* (1), 59–63.

Zaharna, R. S. "Self-Shock: The Double-Binding Challenge of Identity." *International Journal of Intercultural Relations,* 1989, *13* (4), 501–525.

GERALD WEINSTEIN is a professor at the University of Massachusetts School of Education in the Human Development Program, with special interest in the evolution of self-knowledge. He began introducing antiracism instruction in Philadelphia public schools in 1954 and developed the first anti-Semitism workshop for the University of Massachusetts, Amherst, Social Issues Project.

KATHY OBEAR is completing her doctorate in the Social Justice Education Program at the School of Education, University of Massachusetts, Amherst, and is a management consultant (The Human Advantage, Amherst, Mass.).

PART TWO

Social Diversity in the Curriculum

This chapter examines fundamental differences between the fields of international and multicultural education, discussing significant commonalities and areas for collaboration. Successful strategies in teaching and working with multicultural and international students are presented.

International and Multicultural Education: Unrelated Adversaries or Successful Partners?

June Noronha

Traditionally on campus, discussions about enriching the cultural fabric of an institution or broadening the cultural dialogue in the classroom have assumed the introduction of an international dimension. Even with the development of ethnic studies in the seventies, international education continued to be the accepted and familiar approach to diversity. Study about cultures and languages beyond our shores and borders has been woven into our presumptions about cross-cultural learning.

Recently, however, discussions of diversity have been forced by national agendas to reconsider studies of specific domestic cultural groups, and to revive the debate about a multicultural versus an international perspective in the classroom and across the institution. It is not surprising that these two approaches are seen to be separate, different, unrelated to each other, and in some cases adversarial. It is unfortunate, however, because although there are conflicting perspectives between these two fields, there are also significant commonalities for cross-fertilization and collaboration in the areas of cross-cultural and diversity training, for example, or in culture shock and cultural adjustment theories. The fact is that there is a greater body of research in international education, as recorded in the *International Journal of Intercultural Relations,* for example, and there has been more political and financial support on campuses for international education. This history and these resources can only enhance more recent initiatives on multicultural education, which in turn can enrich the entire diversity dialogue by challenging accepted institutional assumptions about cross-cultural learning. Both focus on developing knowledge of the dynamic inherent in cultural interaction and on enhancing the skills that lead, for example, to tolerance, conflict resolution, and behavior transformation. Faculty and administration will increase their effectiveness by understanding these differences and similarities and synthesizing them to improve teaching and administration.

Perspectives on Diversity

The issues are complicated by a lack of campus consensus about what the climate for social and cultural diversity at the university means. At the broadest level, it means attention paid to the social and intellectual life of an institution to support an environment that promotes sensitivity to all groups of people, whether defined by race, ethnicity, religion, gender, sexual orientation, country of origin, or physical disability. These definitions involve very complex issues because they embrace perspectives that straddle many ascribed cultural orientations and often defy categorization. For example, does the term *multicultural* include issues of gender and sexual orientation? Do Asian American lesbians have more in common with communities of color than with other lesbians? Do men as a group have similarities and a culture that transcend ethnic differences? My own opinion is that issues of culture, race, and ethnicity go much deeper than issues of gender, class, sexual orientation, or disability, but that they should not be limited to a narrow representation of the cultural and ethnic perspectives and groups within the campus community that often arise because of political pressures.

The latter perspective results in a fragmented approach to diversity, is ultimately ineffective to transform either the curriculum or campus climate, and does not allow the integration of the full range of relevant theories and practices accumulated in international education research.

International Education

The focus of international education has been on transnational exchanges of ideas and peoples and on the interaction between U.S. and non-U.S. cultures, predominantly between European American and European cultures (see Althen, 1981; Fersh, 1974; Solomon and Young, 1987; Weaver and Wollitzer, 1991). U.S. culture has generally been defined in a traditional, middle-class, European American context, and international students are generally oriented toward that perspective, an interesting dynamic since 88 percent of international students coming to the United States in 1989–90 were from non-European countries.

International education has continued to be isolated within a specific cultural milieu. Although faculty and students have had very diverse experiences in learning, the field rarely deals with explicit or troubling racial or ethnic issues and lacks an overt sociopolitical agenda. Therefore, issues such as the differential treatment of African and Asian students in this country, or race and privilege among Latin American students, or the preference for study in Britain over Brazil, or the romanticizing of international over multicultural education are ignored. Historically, the international studies field has been well funded, research grants and Fulbright awards are available, and language studies are core campus disciplines. International education has a sophisticated body of theory and training methodologies developed by communication theorists and political and social scientists, much of it centered in the field of intercultural communication, which Samovar, Porter, and Jain define as "the systematic study of exactly what happens when cross-cultural contacts and interaction takes place" (1981, p. 4). It has been on the national agenda and assumed to be accessible to all except, until recently, multicultural populations. On campus, therefore, education about things international is more easily funded and supported and, if defined as education about diversity, more readily accepted.

Multicultural Education

The focus here is on issues of privilege, dominance, status differences, and the inter- and intragroup dynamic in this country. It is on ethnic and social differences within national boundaries. It defines U.S. culture as a multiplicity of traditions, with tensions within and among groups. Tensions tend to be explained in the context of the African American experience in this country, perhaps because the African American community has been most vocal in the attempt to broaden the discussion of diversity, and because the definitions of racial issues still tend to be defined narrowly in a Black/White context. Multicultural education has a political analytic base and actively deals with issues of inclusion and exclusion and challenge to the status quo, whereas international education tends to focus on enrichment and adjustment (Banks and Banks, 1989; Bunzel, 1992; Smith, 1989). Most multicultural education theory is applied from the social sciences; it has a growing number of national spokespersons.

International Versus Multicultural Perspectives

For faculty and staff on campus, multicultural education is often assumed to be the business of special interests, separate (with, for example, ethnic studies taught by ethnic faculty, women's studies by women), problematic, more accessible by direct experience than by structured learning, and subject to pressure groups on and off campus. International education on the other hand is thought to be more subject to external

pressures such as global political and economic trends, graduate enrollments, government funding, and the strength or weakness of the U.S.
dollar. Essentially, it is thought to be more accessible by structured
learning than direct experience: if one is committed and interested, it is
assumed that one can teach and learn effectively in the field.

In the pursuit of diversity on campus, the internationalists (predominantly European American) have generally not been engaged or included
in the discussions with multiculturalists (predominantly Americans of
color), and faculty, staff, and students in the two areas do not often work
or plan together. Each area assumes a specific mastery over cultural
learning and is often suspicious and critical of the other's approach,
analysis, and theoretical knowledge. The situation seems to reflect the
dynamics of the larger society, where those who perceive inequities have
to force their agenda on those who shape the institutional agenda.

Multiculturalists tend to perceive internationalists as elitist and interested in esoteric agendas; they are perceived in turn as professional
victims, exclusionary, and theoretically soft. Faculty and staff who do not
work in either of these areas have not found a mechanism to include the
expertise of either group in their own work, and as the dialogue about
diversity on campus becomes more complex, many attempt to steer clear
of potential conflicts.

International students, too, often have little exposure or interaction
with multicultural students; these groups do not often form automatic
alliances or perceive their situations to be related, and, generally speaking, they have different student profiles. International students tend to be
older than the U.S. national norm, from higher socioeconomic stratas of
their home societies, attend full-time, go on to graduate work, and select
traditional fields of letters and science. Multicultural students cannot be
as easily typified, but fewer African Americans and Hispanic Americans,
for example, complete degrees, and their persistence rates in college are
lower than those of other student groups (Carter and Wilson, 1991).

Multicultural students, on their part, often see international students
as politically unaware and privileged; international students tend to not
want to be identified with a perceived disadvantage that groups dealing
with social inequities face. The larger campus community, on the other
hand, often groups diverse populations together simply on the basis of
their difference from the predominantly European American campus
population. This not only hinders classroom learning but fosters major
misunderstandings.

Effective Teaching Strategies

How then do we teach effectively in this environment and use the
resources in the different fields, in the student body and on the faculty

and staff, to contribute to a climate of diversity on campus? Crucial to teaching diverse student populations and working toward a multicultural learning environment is a clear understanding of the tensions and dilemmas facing the diverse populations on campus. Also important is a deliberate effort to include all members of all groups in the exploration, understanding, and appreciation of one another's cultural experiences and heritage.

Effective, high-quality teaching for a diverse population operates on the same principles as good teaching practice for all students; essential to this are students in the role of active learners. In the *Wingspread Journal,* Chickering and Gamson list seven principles for good practice (Chickering and Gamson, 1987; reprinted in Green, 1989). These encourage student-faculty contact, cooperation among students, active learning, giving prompt feedback, emphasis on time on task, communication of high expectations, and respect for diverse talents and ways of learning. Those teaching international and multicultural students need to put these general principles in the perspective of the complex issues that arise from the disparities for multicultural as well as international students between the worlds of their home communities or countries and the college campus (see Pemberton, 1988).

Faculty who wish to improve and enhance their own teaching practice may consider the following principles and related strategies that the author has used successfully in her work:

Improve interpersonal relations with the student or colleague in and out of the classroom (befriend students or colleagues, find out about their classroom or campus experiences, invite them as guest lecturers in their field).

Strengthen the faculty-student relationship.

Learn what subliminal messages about expectations of multicultural or international students you may be communicating. Our expectations are based on our cultural values and experience. Multicultural and some international students often comment that instructors have fewer expectations of them than of other students, although they are often called on to explain international issues, or race relations, or the minority condition and history—in effect forced into the role of resident expert on a topic they have come to class to learn about.

Realize that ethnic visibility makes it challenging to live a normal life on campus. An identifiably different student's absence or presence in class is more noticeable. The current emphasis on cultural sensitivity may lead to unfounded assumptions or unwelcome special treatment. The students themselves are always conscious of not being part of the classroom majority, which affects their perceptions of the learning experience.

Use teaching tools that have been developed for cross-cultural learning, such as small-group projects, first-person accounts, role playing, mini-research, experiential games, activities that break up the class and encourage mixing and interaction, and one-to-one involvements between students and faculty.

Learn more about cross-cultural communication differences (use of silences, eye contact, seating arrangements, male-female behavior, verbal and nonverbal communication) and their effect on learning styles. Introduce a variety of teaching methods to enable different students to succeed in different circumstances.

Appreciate the importance of feedback and encouragement, especially for international and multicultural students, within a context of high expectation. Multicultural students are often bicultural, understand cross-cultural issues, and provide effective cultural bridges as mentors for international students. International students often make effective tutors or group leaders.

Use these students appropriately in the classroom, and encourage mentoring and collaboration with others.

Observe and learn from those who work well with diverse groups of students, drawing on the informal network of information on supportive faculty and staff that often exists among international and multicultural students.

Reach out to international and multicultural faculty and staff, and collaborate for mutual benefit.

Conclusion

International education and multicultural education have much in common and much to contribute to the broadening of diversity in its widest sense on a campus. Faculty and staff in both areas have a commitment to understanding and teaching about cultural interaction, change, and adaptation. Both deal with curricular transformation and extracurricular learning, community building, and supportive environments for retention and graduation. Both study and teach about plural societies with all their complexities, divisions, caste systems, and challenges. The teaching tools used in both these fields have been developed specifically for their effectiveness in cross-cultural learning—that is, understanding and learning about one's own and other's assumptions, values, and behaviors and about what happens when individuals and groups from different cultures interact (see Brislin, 1981; Condon and Yousef, 1975). Tools include role playing, first-person accounts, autobiographies, and experiential games such as Bafa Bafa (Shirts, 1978) and are often the same in both the international and multicultural fields. The theories discussed in the literature in both areas (culture shock, dominant versus nondominant culture, cross-cultural adjustment, assimilation and integration) are similar. Field experiences, culture-contrast surveys, social structure analysis, language study, and racism training are used separately in both areas. Strengthening the alliances among these groups and expanding the boundaries of the discussion will increase the possibility of strategic and long-term change in the classroom and at the institution.

References

Althen, G. (ed.). *Learning Across Cultures.* Washington, D.C.: National Association for Foreign Student Affairs, 1981.

Banks, J. A., and Banks, C.A.M. *Multicultural Education: Issues and Perspectives.* Needham Heights, Mass.: Allyn & Bacon, 1989.

Brislin, R. W. *Cross-Cultural Encounters.* New York: Pergamon Press, 1981.

Bunzel, J. H. *Race Relations on Campus: Stanford Students Speak.* Palo Alto, Calif.: Stanford Alumni Association, 1992.

Carter, D. J., and Wilson, R. *Ninth Annual Status Report on Minorities in Higher Education.* Washington, D.C.: American Council on Education, 1991.

Chickering, A. W., and Gamson, Z. F. "Seven Principles for Good Practice in Undergraduate Education." *Wingspread Journal,* 1987, *9* (2). Special insert.

Condon, J. C., and Yousef, F. S. *An Introduction to Intercultural Communication.* Bobbs-Merrill Series in Speech Communication, no. 19. Indianapolis: Bobbs-Merrill, 1975.

Fersh, S. (ed.). *Learning About Peoples and Cultures.* Evanston, Ill.: McDougal, Littell & Co., 1974.

Green, M. F. (ed.). *Minorities on Campus: A Handbook for Enhancing Diversity.* Washington, D.C.: American Council on Education, 1989.

Pemberton, G. *On Teaching the Minority Student: Problems and Strategies.* Brunswick, Me.: Bowdoin College, 1988.

Samovar, L. A., Porter, R. E., and Jain, N. C. (eds.). *Understanding Intercultural Communication.* Belmont, Calif.: Wadsworth, 1981.

Shirts, R. G. *Bafa Bafa.* Yarmouth, Me.: Intercultural Press, 1978.

Smith, D. G. *The Challenge of Diversity: Involvement or Alienation in the Academy?* ASHE-ERIC Higher Education Reports, no. 5. Washington, D.C.: School of Education and Human Development, George Washington University, 1989.

Solomon, L. C., and Young, B. J. *The Foreign Student Factor: Impact on American Higher Education.* New York: Institute of International Education, 1987.

Weaver, H. D., and Wollitzer, P. A. (eds.). "Internationalizing Higher Education." *American Behavioral Scientist,* 1991, *35* (1). Special issue.

JUNE NORONHA is associate dean for multicultural education at the College of St. Catherine, St. Paul, Minnesota, and conducts international and diversity strategic planning workshops for higher education.

Across the country, faculty members are redefining core knowledge and skills to include learning about U.S. pluralism and world cultures and experimenting with new pedagogical approaches that engage cultural multiplicity in effective ways.

Cultural Pluralism and Core Curricula

Betty Schmitz

More than two decades of new scholarship from American ethnic studies, women's studies, and third world studies have brought new theories, perspectives, and interpretations into prominence in the academy. At the same time, rapid socioeconomic, political, and environmental transformations both within and beyond the borders of the United States have heightened the consciousness of educational leaders to the necessity of preparing students for the new realities of interactions and transactions in an interdependent world of great cultural multiplicity. In the United States, we are struggling to redefine our collective identity, and the stakes are high for both those in the dominant culture and those who have been marginalized.

Faculty members across the country are challenging traditional notions of curricular content and pedagogy. They are asking fundamental questions about what students should know, what they should know how to do, and what kinds of values and habits they need to develop for effective citizenship in a multicultural society. In the process, they are reevaluating approaches to traditional Western canons and redefining core knowledge to include learnings about U.S. pluralism and about other parts of the world.

These changes are reflected in a diversification of curricular choices and requirements. The Carnegie Foundation for the Advancement of Teaching (1992) reports that between 1970 and 1985, the percentage of four-year colleges and universities with general education requirements for at least one course in international or global education increased from 4.5 to 14.6 percent, in third world studies from 2.9 to 7.9 percent, and in women's studies from zero to 1.6 percent. Required courses in the history of Western civilization rose from 43.1 to 48.5 percent. By 1990, 53 percent of institutions required students to take a course in Western civilization, 46 percent in world civilizations, and 20 percent in racial or ethnic content. Levine and Cureton (1992) report that more than one-third of all colleges and universities now have a multicultural require-ment for graduation; at least a third offer course work in ethnic and gender studies; and more than half have introduced multiculturalism into their departmental course offerings. Gaff (1991), in his survey of trends in general education reform, found that global affairs and cultural diversity were two top trends campus leaders thought would influence curricular change at their own institutions in the 1990s.

These changes have not come about without contest, however, as reports in the national and academic press over the past few years indicate. There is by no means consensus nationally or on any campus about the kind or degree of curriculum change that is required to attend to issues of diversity. While institutional mission statements have been revised to include statements valuing cultural pluralism, and while ad-ministrators support these efforts to varying degrees, it is the faculty members themselves who struggle with the conceptual and pedagogical tasks of engaging difference in the classroom. As teachers and as program directors, they are the ones who bear the primary responsibility for shaping a new curriculum for a new world.

This essay explores institutional and conceptual issues central to addressing cultural pluralism in the core curriculum and describes prac-tices that have proved useful to faculty members developing or revising courses or planning new curricula. Observations are based primarily on a study of approaches used by faculty members and core curriculum plan-ners in the project "Engaging Cultural Legacies: Shaping Core Curricula in the Humanities," sponsored by the Association of American Colleges with a grant from the National Endowment for the Humanities (Schmitz, 1992). Project resources supported a total of fifty-four institutions creat-ing or revising core curricula to engage the multiplicity of cultural legacies.

Cultural Pluralism: The Challenges of Content

Models, Choices, Issues. Faculty members eager to bring the study of cultural pluralism into undergraduate education encounter two models for the integration of new content: (1) the development of new interdis-ciplinary fields that focus on the study of previously marginalized groups— American ethnic studies, women's studies, third world studies, and the intersections of these fields; and (2) the integration of theory, content, and pedagogy of these fields into courses across the general education or core curriculum. The first approach, an additive one, has contributed to the ongoing development of new scholarship and scholarly fields within the academy that focus on the traditions and histories of diverse cultures and civilizations. This base of scholarship provides an indispensable foundation for the attempts to address cultural pluralism in the core curriculum proper. Courses within these curricula have served as a means for students interested in cultural diversity to pursue this study and also as requirements for departmental majors that view this knowledge as essential. The additive model does not, however, address the need to create a common experience of exploring cultural pluralism for all students.

It may also perpetuate conceptual confusions about the study of multiculturalism. Often disparate courses are added to a "multicultural" menu when political compromises rather than student learning goals dictate curricular choices. Distinct content areas may be combined, as in lumping together all "otherness" by requiring students to take a course on minority groups in the United States or a course on women or a course on non-Western culture. A course on Chinese philosophy has educational purposes that are quite different from those implicit in a course on Native American women, and both differ fundamentally from a course that engages students in the study of racism, sexism, anti-Semitism, homophobia, and other forms of prejudice and discrimination. Any or all of these courses may provide valuable learning experiences for students at a particular campus, but they attend to very different learning goals. Students hardly learn what they need to know about U.S. populations of color from taking a course about a "non-Western" civilization.

The second approach, the incorporation of the study of cultural multiplicity into the courses in the core curriculum, brings the new studies into a central place in the academy. When multiple cultural traditions with powerful and cohesive stories, but unequal status in the academy, encounter one another in a course, faculty members must rethink older paradigms for the study of civilizations and cultures and explore ways to connect the values and experiences of disparate human societies across time and place.

Numerous content choices present themselves to core curriculum planners thinking about culture, cultural legacies, and cultural relations: which Western themes and texts to include in the core curriculum; where and how to include study of so-called non-Western cultures; where and how to include the study of U.S. pluralism or multiculturalism; and how to address race, gender, ethnicity, class, sexual orientation, and other constructed dimensions of human identity within the core. The intensity of discussions results both from the compelling intellectual task of sorting out the multiple dimensions of cultural pluralism and from the transformative power of the new fields of study as students and faculty members engage them.

Choices are further complicated by the history of national and campus discussions about multiculturalism. The term *multicultural* is now often used simultaneously to refer to the study of African, Asian, Middle Eastern, Latin American, and other "world" cultures and to the study of minority cultures within the United States. Yet until recently, the term referred only to the study of U.S. populations of color. Some faculty members believe that exposure to any other country's culture, history, or language is sufficient; others insist that students must learn to analyze cultural relations in terms of power. That is, when and why does difference mean dominance of one culture over another? Curriculum planners who wish to teach all students about prejudice, discrimination, and the "isms" have adopted requirements that all students take a course on these topics.

Misconceiving and Misrepresenting the "Other." Most recent discussions about content choices have centered on the proper due to be given to Western traditions in core programs. Responses could be arranged on a continuum: teaching the West or its great texts without reference to other traditions, which are relegated to a special requirement in non-Western studies; teaching it centrally while consciously exploring the critical traditions within it and purposefully comparing it to other cultural traditions; or teaching it as one tradition to be studied among many.

Comparative models run the risk of privileging one group over another and, in the process, misrepresenting other cultures, as when cultural paradigms chosen to organize a course define a priori other cultures only through Western eyes. For example, a course might be structured to look at the "golden age" of a particular culture, then the moment the culture comes under stress from Western colonialism, and then the culture's response to Western influence or control. Another similarly problematic approach involves requiring that students get a solid base in Western culture first, or study a social science, or both, before looking at "nondominant" or "minority" cultures. The message here is that Western culture is timeless, above societal pressures and idiosyncracies, whereas other cultures are born out of social and political pressures, embedded in the immediacy of historical moments, and hence not universally meaningful.

Still another approach is the introduction of other groups for the purpose of elucidating the value of the dominant tradition through comparison. The second culture studied becomes defined, not as a presence in and of itself, but as an absence or negation of mainstream culture. In developing their world cultures course, faculty members at one large state university came to realize that they might unintentionally reinforce existing stereotypes by maintaining as separate and inviolable categories "West" and "non-West." Such a rigid distinction would allow students to continue to think in terms of "us" and "them," "we" being "natural" and "they" being "exotic and strange." This result would defeat one of the principal aims of curriculum reform—to foster in students greater sensitivity to cultural pluralism.

Viewing the contributions and experiences of different cultural groups from the perspective of the mainstream may also define the groups studied as powerless, focusing on the "plight" of these groups or their "special problems." Even with analyses of structures of domination with the intent of illuminating the reasons for power and status differentials, the overall effect may be less than desirable. Students from the dominant culture may feel guilty and defensive, and exhibit denial or anger, while students from the "oppressed" groups may react negatively to literature that puts them at the center but casts them as victim.

Unidimensionality is another way of misrepresenting cultures. Often faculty members will introduce new content that reflects only one of the many dimensions of diversity—ethnicity, race, national origin, or gender. Thus we have new courses in world civilizations that pay no attention to gender or new courses on gender as if it were the only category of female experience. Age, disability, and sexual orientation rarely appear on syllabi fulfilling general education requirements and those that have this kind of analysis tend to be developed by faculty members in the new interdisciplinary fields of women's or ethnic studies.

Curricular Solutions

Multiple Centers. To avoid such unintended messages when studying cultures comparatively, Butler and Schmitz (1991) suggest exploring a concept of multiple centers (traditions, perspectives, bodies of knowledge), rather than a single center that supposedly encompasses all. The concept of multiple centers allows the foregrounding of a specific group or tradition without the obscuration of the others that words such as *decentering* and *re-centering* suggest. Reflecting reality, these centers overlap: they represent the multiplicity of individuals and groups, shared heritages and traditions, influences, borrowings, and legacies. Inquiry draws on all disciplines, generating interdisciplinary connections. Interdependent margins and centers share space within a multidimensional framework.

In such an approach, different voices may occupy the center of attention for specific times; they are studied on their own terms, as viewed from within the culture. Traditions and cultures, Western and world, are viewed critically but not judgmentally. For other purposes and at other times, themes might be chosen to compare cultures and illuminate differing worldviews and perspectives.

Examples from the Engaging Cultural Legacies Project illustrate how comparative approaches could situate U.S., Western, and world traditions within larger, encompassing narratives. The use of themes as an organizing principle proved an excellent means to situate diverse cultures within their own worldviews and cultural constructs. Themes are used to examine generative periods in selected cultures; to connect texts and topics from different cultures that may not necessarily be contemporary; to explore fundamental dimensions of human experience such as faith, virtue, and memory; to introduce interdisciplinary or multidisciplinary perspectives; or to incorporate race, class, gender, and ethnicity into the curriculum.

Students at Tufts University choose from among three two-semester thematically organized sequences of world civilizations: "A Sense of Place," "Time and Calendars," and "Memory and Identity in World Cultures." The themes allow cross-cultural analysis through a sampling of at least three cultures. For example, in a representative second-semester section of the course "Memory and Identity," students explore their interplay by looking at four case studies: the Atlanta slave trade and the construction of African Caribbean identity in Haiti; the western expansion of white settlement in America and its effects on Cherokee society; the construction of religious identity and communalism in British India leading up to the partition of India and Pakistan in 1947; and struggles over the construction of social and cultural identity in colonial and postcolonial Kenya.

A faculty member at LeMoyne-Owen College opens her section of the "Human Heritage" core course by having students examine art and writings from traditional African and Asian cultures: an eighth-century Chinese tomb ornament representing a saddled camel; a West African headdress representing two antelopes, a smaller one on the back of a larger one; a tenth-century Chinese ink painting of a mountain and valley entitled "Festival of the Rain"; Ashanti proverbs; a passage on ethics and politics from Confucius; a tenth-century neo-Confucian poem, "Song of Happiness"; and other cultural artifacts. The students' task is to learn what they can about the worldview of these cultures by examining these different "texts." In discussing the texts as manifestations of cultural worldviews, students are discouraged from making judgments about the relative worth of the texts or elaborate comparisons among them. They concentrate on "reading" the text and drawing hypotheses that they can test in more detail as the course proceeds.

"World Cultures and Traditions," a course being piloted at the University of Oklahoma, presents humanities texts from at least three different world cultures. In the first semester, organized around common themes, a "universal" aspect of human experience (for example, the passage from childhood to adulthood, illness and death) anchors discussion of the topics. Looking at values and worldviews as elements of culture, students read texts as diverse as the *Aeneid,* eighteenth-century Chinese maxims for daily life, and selections from Alice Walker, Zora

Neale Hurston, and Nietzsche's *The Birth of Tragedy.* The second semester examines historical change in economic, political, and social systems and the dynamics of interaction between and among groups with different backgrounds and cultures.

In developing a core humanities sequence, faculty planners at institutions that envisage including both world cultures and U.S. pluralism frequently debate the benefits for students of starting with the "Ancients" rather than with contemporary issues. The year-long introductory core course "Crossroads" at the University of Wyoming begins with the present and uses this metaphor as an ongoing principle for the course. Unit I, "The Land," begins with the local context and explores conflicts between European American and American Indian concepts and between environmentalists and multiple-use advocates' interpretations of land use. Unit II, "The Hero," explores conceptions about heroes in contemporary U.S. culture, in the Western European heritage, and in non-Western tradition. Units III and IV, "Urban and Rural Cultures" and "Equality," also juxtapose texts from different times and cultures.

Many colleges and universities are extending core study over several courses in order to attend to the range of cultural multiplicity. Fairleigh Dickinson University, for example, has a four-course sequence that moves from study of the individual, to study of American cultural legacies, to cross-cultural study of five civilizations, and finally to a course on global issues. At Samford University, the core includes a year-long sequence in European traditions, which includes the study of cultural interactions, such as Islam during the Crusades; a year-long course devoted to the study of African, East Asian, and Middle Eastern cultures, and a year-long course, "The American Experience," that covers both Latin and North American cultures.

New Pedagogies. Ethnic studies and women's studies faculty are critical sources of energy and enthusiasm for new pedagogical approaches because of their history of student-centered teaching and learning. The early stages of feminist and black studies pedagogy sought to build on experiences familiar to specific student populations. Influenced by Paolo Freire and others, faculty members developed teaching practices that valued the individual student's experience as a base of knowledge to complement textual materials, attempted to break down hierarchical modes of teaching, and taught students to take responsibility for their own learning.

Models for collaborative learning gained considerable ground in the early eighties. Collaborative learning emphasizes both social and intellectual engagement and responsibility in an attempt to counteract many current ills of college teaching: the distance between faculty members and students, overreliance on the lecture method, the passivity of students and their alienation from one another and the learning process

(Smith and MacGregor, 1992). One of the benefits of this new paradigm is a kind of parity between student and faculty: Each one recognizes that the perspectives and experience of the other will contribute to the process of teaching and learning (Romer, 1985).

The introduction of new cultural histories has provided an optimum situation for new pedagogies. New core curriculum programs incorporating cultural pluralism are staffed primarily by faculty members who have gained their expertise in these materials through recent faculty development activities. They themselves are students of new subject matter that does not fit within the boundaries of familiar domains. They are forming learning communities with peers in other fields and departments who staff new core courses.

Faculty members and curriculum planners are experimenting in deliberate and systematic ways with interdisciplinary and thematic approaches, with new forms of student interaction and involvement in the learning process, and with connecting learning across courses and across curricula. In this mode, faculty members act more as facilitators than experts. Their role is to guide students in their exploration of texts, not to predefine what is of interest and importance. They allow students to see their own learning processes in the way they handle questions: "I don't know the answer to that question, but this might be a part of it. I'll check and see what I can find."

At the University of Richmond, faculty members in the core program make heavy use of collaborative learning activities, for example, small group work in which students generate central questions about the readings. They make no secret of the fact that they are co-learners with the students and that they are working together to explore questions raised by the texts. In interviews, faculty members praised the new methods as more intellectually stimulating and rewarding for students, who practice skills in summary, critique, analysis, and theory building, all of which are viewed as fundamental to the continuation of their learning in their undergraduate years and beyond.

These new pedagogies, common in the Engaging Cultural Legacies Project, indicate a noticeable shift on many campuses in attitudes about student learning in the classroom. Faculty members are changing their ideas about content acquisition and are seeing the inefficacy of blaming students for what they do not know and do not value. They are beginning to see their role as helping students connect the course content with what students do know and care about, including themselves. These developments portend well for student learning outcomes. Astin (1992) and Pascarella and Terenzini (1991) have demonstrated that all of these practices correlate positively with students' intellectual development and maturation in college.

The resonance between the role of faculty member as facilitator or master learner, rather than expert, and the new focus on the individual as interdependent with the community in the Engaging Cultural Legacies Project, is no accident. With collaborative learning activities and redefinition of the place of individual effort, the paradigm of the individual central to the Western tradition is coming into question. This shift toward valuing one's connection to and responsibility to others and cooperative modes of interaction, if it continues, will be a welcome relief from the norms of aggressive individualism, competitiveness, and self-centeredness that currently characterize much of our society. This new mode of teaching/learning will also help prepare students for living in a multicultural society. To accomplish that aim, however, faculties must commit themselves to begin their review of the curriculum by defining their goals for student learning—knowledge, skills, and civic competencies—and identifying the content areas and pedagogical strategies that lead to those learning outcomes.

References

Astin, A. W. *What Matters in College? Four Critical Years Revisited.* San Francisco: Jossey-Bass, 1992.

Butler, J. E., and Schmitz, B. "Transforming the Curriculum: Incorporating Different Voices." Workshop delivered at the conference Ourselves Among Others sponsored by the Washington Center for Undergraduate Education, Seattle, Washington, February 1, 1991.

Carnegie Foundation for the Advancement of Teaching. "Signs of a Changing Curriculum." *Change,* 1992, 24 (1), 49–52.

Gaff, J. G. *New Life for the College Curriculum: Assessing Achievements and Furthering Progress in the Reform of General Education.* San Francisco: Jossey-Bass, 1991.

Levine, A., and Cureton, J. "The Quiet Revolution: Eleven Facts About Multiculturalism and the Curriculum." *Change,* 1992, 24 (1), 25–29.

Morris, M. "A Work in Progress: The New Civic Competencies." Paper presented at the National Society for Internships and Experiential Education, Santa Fe, N.Mex., Oct. 27, 1989.

Pascarella, E. T., and Terenzini, P. T. *How College Affects Students: Findings and Insights from Twenty Years of Research.* San Francisco: Jossey-Bass, 1991.

Romer, K. T. "Collaboration: New Forms of Learning, New Ways of Thinking." *The Forum for Liberal Education,* 1985, 8 (2), 2–4.

Schmitz, B. *Core Curricula and Cultural Legacies.* Washington, D.C.: Association of American Colleges, 1992.

Smith, D. L., and MacGregor, J. T. "What is Collaborative Learning?" In A. Goodsell and others (eds.), *A Sourcebook on Collaborative Learning in Higher Education.* University Park, Penn.: National Center on Postsecondary Teaching, Learning and Assessment, 1992.

BETTY SCHMITZ is codirector, Cultural Pluralism Project, University of Washington, and senior project associate, Washington Center for Improving the Quality of Undergraduate Education, Evergreen State College.

Today's challenge, for students and teachers of writing alike, is to construct a social identity on which we can all agree—whether it is the page of a text, the way we teach it, or the way students compose texts of their "own"—amid a growing confluence of identities, both individual and ethnic.

Diversity in Required Writing Courses

Marcia S. Curtis, Anne J. Herrington

The instructor said,

> *Go home and write*
> *a page tonight.*
> *And let that page come out of you—*
> *Then, it will be true.*

I wonder if it's that simple?

Posing that question over a half century ago, the African American poet Langston Hughes (1951) situated a central dilemma of postwar adolescence and early adulthood within the particular context of a Columbia University writing class. Attempting to resolve it, he articulated another question and a truth that have become the central dilemma and broad debate of educators in the 1990s:

> . . . will my page be colored that I write?
> Being me, it will not be white.
> But it will be

We acknowledge and thank these graduate student instructors, on whose advice we have so heavily relied in constructing our curriculum: Sartaz Aziz, Lou Berney, William Clements, James Garman, Marci Goodman, Sabine Groote, Mary Hess, Christine Hoekstra, Amy Hoffman, Susan Hyatt, Emily Isaacs, Jean Jeffries, Elizabeth Klem, Amy Lee, Jun Liu, Anne Mullin, Erin Murphy, Paul Puccio, Josna Rege, Perrin Reid, Nancy Reisman, Erika Scheurer, and Barbara Tannert.

> a part of you, instructor.
> You are white—
> yet a part of me, as I am a part of you.
> That's American.
>   —"Theme for English B" [Hughes, 1951]

In that Columbia classroom, the problem was Hughes's: to construct a personal identity amid a torrent of conflicting influences. Today, the challenge is to all of us, students and teachers alike: to construct a social identity on which we can all agree—whether it is the page of a text, the way we teachers teach it, or the way our students compose texts of their "own"—amid a growing confluence of identities, individual and ethnic.

What has changed since the publication of Hughes's "Theme" is the balance of demographics or, perhaps more accurately, our perception of their significance, which in itself is enough to tip the balance. When Hughes attended Columbia for a year in the early 1920s, he was, as he says, "the only colored student in my class" (1951, line 10). Today the definition of students of color has changed, and so have their proportionate numbers. We are all by now no doubt well aware of the federal Census Bureau's prediction that by the year 2005, 52 percent of this country's population will be "minority" (if that term can still sensibly be applied), and one out of three students will be of color. For some in the teaching profession, the year 2005 has already arrived.

This is certainly the case for those of us teaching the Basic Writing classes of the University of Massachusetts, Amherst, and, according to most reports, for others teaching in various preparatory and developmental writing programs across the nation. Basic Writing annually serves some 250 students, approximately 7 percent of the entering class, whom we judge, on the basis of a placement test, underprepared for our main first-year writing course, College Writing. Depending on the semester, second-language English (SLE) speakers make up between 20 percent and 60 percent of the group, spring semester classes drawing largely on graduates from the university's SLE program. Of those students, the majority comprises nearly equal percentages of Cambodian, Central and South American, Chinese, Japanese, Puerto Rican, Soviet, and Taiwanese students, either visiting or now living in Massachusetts and neighboring states. Of the first-language English speakers, about 30 percent are African American, and a significant portion are children of second-language English speakers from homes in which two languages are spoken. Of the entire group, between 10 percent and 15 percent come to us with diagnosed learning disabilities involving reading and writing. Over the course of a semester, some 30 percent generally disclose histories of parental abandonment or death as well as alcoholism, drug abuse, and violence in their families or to themselves. We presume at least 10 percent of our population, like the population at large, to be gay, lesbian, or bisexual.

These are the students who enter the University of Massachusetts academic community generally, and academic discourse community in particular, through Basic Writing. Since they are our students now, it is for them that we designed the multicultural Basic Writing curriculum and pedagogy currently in place at the Amherst campus. Since they represent the general student body as it soon will be, we believe that many of the principles and practices developed specifically for marginalized writers will apply to mainstream classes of the very near future. Finally, insofar as the multicultural profile of our basic writers—in all their ethnic, racial, and linguistic diversity—may simply bring into relief differences obscured or overlooked among apparently monocultural students—differences of religious belief, sexual orientation, family language, or learning style—we believe that the lessons our work with this group has taught us can be instructive for other teachers, now and in the future.

Beginnings in a Neutral Curriculum

As originally defined, Basic Writing was meant to provide underprepared students with both the self-assurance and the writing skills needed to succeed in the university. Until 1986, it was structured on a highly individualized workshop model designed and popularized by the late Roger Garrison of Westbrook College (Portland, Maine). Following a prescribed process of brainstorming, drafting, and revising, students worked their way through a series of essay assignments arising out of personal experience, without a reader or any text other than the students' own writing. Class time was devoted wholly to writing and student-teacher conferencing; there was no (intended) interaction among class members at all.

By 1986, however, some five years into our program's development, we increasingly sensed that our curriculum, although it enhanced the students' confidence as writers, did not adequately prepare them for the sort of writerly independence fostered and valued in the composition course they would next enter, College Writing. Nor did it prepare them for the reading-based, rather than experience-based, writing demanded in most other college courses. Consequently, we set out to reformulate Basic Writing to fit our general Freshman Writing Program's guiding principles of a student-centered, activity-based curriculum and pedagogy, and also to fit both our basic writers' profile, as we saw it, and what we sensed from experience or knew from research to be expected of writers within academe.

At present, traditional assumptions about valued ways of writing in school and college settings are being questioned (Elbow, 1991; Brodkey, 1987; Bleich, 1988) and with them the aims for basic writing courses. Should such courses aim primarily to impart formal skills? Should they aim to introduce students to the linguistic and intellectual conventions of the academic discourse community? Should they aim to validate the students' own cultural discourses and help students reflect critically on the many and varied discourses in which they are asked to participate? The debates are as numerous as the debaters (Rose, 1983; Bartholomae, 1986; Fox, 1990; Belanoff, 1990; Harris, 1989; Henning, 1991; Hull, Rose, Fraser, and Castellano, 1991). For our own purposes, we settled on the following assumptions. We could neither ascribe to a heavy-handed socialization approach nor accept academic discourse as all of a kind. We could, however, identify certain essential intellectual capacities, beyond a grasp of standard English-language conventions, that most college instructors value in student writers: to be able to move beyond a simple repetition of knowledge gleaned from reading, listening, or observation to more complex interpretation of such information, and to be able to communicate that interpretation to an audience reasonably and effectively, acknowledging—at least implicitly—the existence of other possible interpretations by other writers and by their own readers as well. In essence, we believed that what was wanted of our writers was that they be able to move confidently and thoughtfully through private meaning making to significant communication with others. That ability should be a central aim of our course.

Given these expectations, we made some inferences about our students, inferences that are consistent with those presented by Bartholomae and Petrosky (1986) and that have become the foundation of Basic Writing's new design. (1) As readers, basic writers are often not "bad readers" so much as they are submissive readers, yielding themselves to the text, any text, instead of struggling to participate in it and make it their own. Therefore, they need help in maintaining an open dialogue with the text before them; in focusing on what they remember from their reading, not on what they forget; in recognizing the significance of those points remembered and in making meaning from them by drawing inferences, establishing connections, and discerning the patterns of meaning formed. (2) Active reading is in itself a type of silent revision. Therefore, as writers, our students benefit from the use of texts not as models of writing but as objects for the sort of interpretive analysis they can gradually begin applying both to other readings and to their own writing. (3) As Basic Writing instructors, then, our primary purpose is not to provide students with professional models they cannot possibly emulate or literary forms that we "teach" them either to criticize or to appreciate, but to help them move through private experience into ideas of more general audience interest by making the fundamental connection between themselves and the world—the world, that is, of both the written texts and their own readership beyond.

Establishing a Richly Textured, Comprehensive Curriculum

In the main, we meant the new curriculum to level for our writers the terrain between what they wrote and what they read: we meant to teach them to use writing as a means of opening printed texts to further and different avenues of exploration and reading as a pretext for further writing of their own; offer them authors with whom they might empathize or argue, who could stimulate response from our students and even function as imagined audience for their self-expressions; finally, prompt them to apply the same interpretive and elaborative techniques to their own drafts as they moved through the revising process.

Thus we began broadening our original experience-based writing focus to a reading-based writing course, following in general the propositions presented by Bartholomae and Petrosky (1986). We began as well to foster the students' independence and to suppress the teacher's presence as much as possible by supplementing student-teacher conferences with regular and ongoing peer-review sessions. As we began selecting readings for our restructured course and designing the particular components of its curriculum—reading guides, writing guides, and specific assignments—we recognized almost immediately the real implications of our task. We could not construct a truly student-centered writing curriculum without installing representatives of these students, our students, at its core. Nor could we honestly expect them to enter a discourse community of academic writers without our first demonstrating to them a community of writers in which they are, indeed, welcome. In other words, we could hardly expect students to make themselves writers without first imagining themselves as writers, without first being allowed to see their own images among other writers' images. Were we, as two Anglo women, traditionally educated and middle class, to select their readings and writings out of our background or out of the traditional composition reader canon to which we had become habituated, we would have created a curriculum in our image perhaps, in the university's image certainly, but decidedly not in theirs.

We simply could not risk the significance such a selection might hold. Over the past five years or so, a number of fine multicultural readers have become available to secondary school and college-level composition teachers (Beaty and Hunter, 1989; Gillespie and Singleton, 1991; Hirschberg, 1992; Lauter and others, 1990; Layton, 1991; Rico and Mano, 1991; Verburg, 1988). However, one need only skim the contents of any of the multitude of traditional composition readers available in 1986, and still available on many campuses, to read a message there: George Orwell, John Ciardi, Tom Wolfe, Jonathan Kozol, Robert Pirsig, Paul Theroux, and John Updike, to name but a few. All of them are, without question, fine men and writers, but taken together they constitute for minority students a message every bit as politicized as the message of multiculturalism, and potentially far more pedagogically destructive. However expansive their writings, however universal their sentiments and ideals, their presence in our anthologies inscribes a "text" with its own clear meaning: these men are writers of our times; these men are *the* writers of our times; these men represent the single group allowed publicly to express themselves. They are a group to which minority students and women—the majority of our students—do not belong.

It is perhaps worth emphasizing here that it was our primary intention, not to use pedagogy to further any single political agenda, but, quite the contrary, to understand the politics of curriculum development and canon formation in order to further pedagogical goals. This is not to say that "agenda-driven" curricula are wrong, or that our curriculum is apolitical. It is simply to say that our primary intention was not political. It is also to make the somewhat less simple claim that as teachers we have come to recognize all our actions as inescapably political. We make a political decision when we make the apparently instructional choice between, on the one hand, proffering up to our students a literary classic on which to model their own writings and, on the other hand, encouraging them to enter interactive dialogue with a text with which they can grapple, argue, and ultimately identify. It is also a political decision when we choose the texts themselves: a novel by J. D. Salinger or one by the Chinese American writer Amy Tan; a tale of the colonies by George Orwell or a song of Harlem by Langston Hughes. In our case, we made the latter choice almost every time, because a basic tenet of our Freshman Writing Program was to provide a student-centered course of composition study, and in Basic Writing that meant moving minority voices in from the margins.

Thus we chose writers a significant number of whom would be considered outside the Anglo American canon, esteemed writers such as Amy Tan (1990), Michael Dorris (1988), Maxine Hong Kingston (1989a, 1989b), Grace Paley (1987), Richard Rodriguez (1982), Alice Walker (1973, 1976), David Leavitt (1986), John Edgar Wideman (1984), along with E. L. Doctorow (1976) and Donald Barthelme (1974). We chose readings by these authors—both short texts and novel-length "Reading Project" books—that formed a discernible pattern and progression charting the coming-of-age process and the vicissitudes of adolescence and young adulthood: acclaimed works such as Kingston's *China Men* (1989a), Paley's "The Loudest Voice" (1987), and Wideman's *Brothers and Keepers* (1984), along with Doctorow's *Ragtime* (1976) and Barthelme's "The

School" (1974). Most deal with attempts by the writers and their characters to interpret and make meaning of themselves and their surroundings; many deal with the acculturation process, as groups and individuals struggle to accommodate new ways of being and speaking while preserving old identities; a number explore dysfunctional family and educational systems and, alternatively, the losses and rewards that accompany socially prescribed success.

Along with the readings, we designed two different types of assignments meant to introduce our basic writers to the uses of writing as a private means to discovery and as a means to public communication. We intended both types of writing to stir them out of their own narrow perspectives, while simultaneously awakening in them a sense of their own potential authority.

The first type of assignment, short "Guided Writings," is given during and after each reading. Made up of three, four or five "prompts," the Guided Writings represent the workhorses of writing, private process writings that students use to explore the readings and their own thoughts about them. They encourage students to see themselves as equal to the professional writer, engaged in a dialogue of equal authorities, while at the same time uncovering a particular compositional technique: "Imagine that Maxine Hong Kingston is a member of this workshop and explain to her what you believe is the single most important detail of her description of her parents in 'Shaman' " (1989b, pp. 57–61). They encourage students to explore multiple interpretations of a text, including some that may be a source of conflict, even prejudice, in the students themselves: "In Grace Paley's 'The Loudest Voice,' Shirley Abramowitz's parents and neighbors disagree about Shirley's participation in the school's Christmas play. If you were a parent, which side of the argument would you take? Which side do you think your own parents or neighbors might take?" They may ask students to evaluate the validity of a writer's claim by applying it to their own lives: "When in 'Aria' Richard Rodriguez writes, 'It is not possible for a child, any child, ever to use his family's language in school. Not to understand this is to misunderstand the public uses of schooling and to trivialize the nature of intimate life' [1982, p. 12], his ideas reach beyond bilingual education to 'a child, any child.' Explain how they apply to you."

In addition to helping students explore the readings, the Guided Writings are intended to lead them into the second type of writing, that is, longer "public" essays grown out of personal reactions to the given texts but now grown into ideas of wider appeal. The students are free to develop their own topics out of each unit's readings and either to use their individual experiences to help elucidate the ideas and experiences set forth in the texts or to use the texts to help express experiences and ideas of their own. In the main, they write on topics all students know well and can handle with true authority: leaving home and parents; entering a new and diverse world; taking on the learning, language, and identity bestowed by their educational community. Some of them, first- and second-language English speakers alike, through their writing come to recognize their bond with other immigrants and second-language speakers undergoing assimilation into the strange world of academic discourse. And some, both native and nonnative English speakers, by analyzing and empathizing with the struggles of second-language speak- ers to master English, become more attuned to and appreciative of that language's special nuances of sound and structure. Finally, by writing for one another about their cultural differences and across those differences, all our students, we think, become more aware of audience and, just as important, the apparent distance across which their own writerly voices can reach.

Establishing a More Inclusive, Truly Student-Centered Pedagogy

In establishing a pedagogy, an actual approach to teaching the new Basic Writing curriculum, we considered its situation within the Freshman Writing Program, the fundamental tenets of which are that it be a stu- dent-centered writing program in which student writing constitutes the principal activity and student writings the principal texts. We consid- ered, too, the limitations of the course itself: it is a one-semester, three- credit composition course, meeting five class hours or 250 minutes a week. Within these parameters, we needed to make certain choices regarding Basic Writing's aims and goals. Although we had introduced outside texts, ours would remain first and foremost a writing, not a reading, course. And although we designed our Guided Writings to lead students into analyzing closely what they had read, discovering issues and problems raised by their readings and making connections between their own experiences and those represented by the writers before them, we would not devote class time to exercises in reading comprehension or discussions of textual analysis. Instead, we would trust our original assumption in redesigning the curriculum to be true, that like all writers, basic writers need to begin focusing on what they remember from their reading, understanding the reasons those particular points are memo- rable to them, and articulating an interpretation of the texts or issues raised in the texts based on that understanding. We would entrust to our students' writing processes the realization of that assumption.

The decision to foreground student writing and background teacher- led reading discussions had a philosophic as well as a pragmatic base. If our classes were truly to be open to a diversity of student experiences and views, and if, moreover, we were to teach our students themselves to be open to a diversity of perspectives among their readers, then we had to resist the very natural urge of teachers to impose their own readings on both texts and students (Hull and Rose, 1990; Roemer, 1987). More to the point, as traditionally trained English teachers with traditional backgrounds in literary criticism, we had to fight consciously against the pull to make this writing course a literature course. Similarly, as teachers with a not-so-traditional interest in multiculturalism and diversity, we had to fight the pull to make this an "issues" course, reminding ourselves—through our established pedagogy—that what was critical to our mission was not so much the written message but the quality of the writing and diversity of the writers. In fact, the newness of our chosen texts, which were often as essentially foreign to us as to our students, helped us preserve our original intent. Exploring their contents, we necessarily became conscious of our own interpretive processes, and it was these processes, rather than the interpretations, that we meant to pass on to our students.

Thus students spend most of their time, both in and out of class, in workshop fashion, independently reading and writing on a networked computer system. The curriculum is made up of six units, three units containing an average of three brief readings and their corresponding Guided Writings, leading to an essay of two to four pages; two units devoted to essays of similar length developed out of the Reading Project; and a final unit in which students collect and revise their previous essays, producing a desktop publication of their collected works—their *oeuvres*—complete with an introduction of themselves as writers and a preface to each individual entry.

In keeping with the Freshman Writing Program's emphasis on the writing process, students in Basic Writing are encouraged to use their Guided Writings as a form of prewriting or brainstorming before actually drafting their essays. The essays themselves are taken through a series of revisions, punctuated by self-assessment and peer-review sessions in which students reflect and comment on their own and one another's drafts. Finished essays are generally read aloud in class-long reading sessions, published in class collections, and ultimately commented on by the teacher.

Interstudent exchanges of drafts and completed papers are intended to foster self-reflection during the composing process and simultaneously to extend the students' sense of audience beyond the teacher alone. With only a modicum of modeling and practice, students join their teacher in providing one another with a new and responsive—rather than corrective—readership, of the sort that stimulates more, and ultimately more effective, communication—of the sort provided by family and friends a few generations ago, when letter writing was fashionable.

We should perhaps explain here that in the same way that we resist imposing our own interpretations on our students' reading, we also resist imposing our own interpretations on their writings and our own styles on their composing processes. As we train ourselves and our students to be receptive to other perspectives and ideas, we emphasize receptivity and empathy in response to others' written forms. It is not that we eschew either critical thinking or standard language skills. It is that we believe writing—active, engaged, and plentiful writing—must precede the refinement of writing skills. And trust in one's audience's willingness to receive information, as much as in one's ability to communicate it, must precede all else.

Speaking of Similarity: Writing Across Difference

In evaluating our curriculum, we depend principally on our students, on the writing they do, and on the vision they present of themselves as they do it. Before letting individuals speak for themselves, we will make just two broad observations. The first is that our original intention in establishing a multicultural curriculum was to offer marginalized students and second-language English speakers opportunity to take on authority roles, at least in relation to their own culture-specific texts. Since that beginning, however, our intention has changed. For Asian students often do take delight in explaining the background of Kingston's or Tan's writings, and Latino students are often looked to by their classmates for special knowledge of Richard Rodriguez's memoir of a bilingual childhood. But for the most part, it is a sort of similarity across difference, rather than direct identity, that students seek out and explore: most students, as we will soon show, choose to read and write about texts from cultures other than their own, and it is a sense of identity discovered across borders that seems to provoke greatest reading delight and writing satisfaction.

A second understanding has come to us with equal surprise. It is that students seldom, if ever, mention the diverse nature of our Basic Writing "canon," seldom attend to the multicultural aspect of our curriculum, which seemed so obvious, new, and central to us. On reflection the reason is, of course, clear: multiculturalism is their culture. Its existence is as transparent as it is natural to them—far more transparent, we suspect, than the all-white canonical hue of tradition. Thus, as the comments that follow illustrate, students may refer to the readings, but almost never in isolation. Rather, they comment on the readings as occasions for writing, and particular occasions for writerly success. That, we believe, is as it should be.

The first illustration appears in the final oeuvre of José Belliard and prefaces his Reading Project essays. Born in the United States but having spent the greater part of his youth in his ancestral homeland, the Dominican Republic, Belliard chose to read and write about Rodriguez's recollections of a Mexican American childhood, *Hunger of Memory* (1982). In doing so, he establishes with Rodriguez a fixed set of commonalities, but by his very deliberate effort reminds us that these are similarities extracted from fundamental differences between persons of Mexican and Dominican descent that we "majority" teachers, in our self-conscious awareness of "minority" groups, are all too apt to forget. Belliard writes:

> I have selected [*Hunger of Memory*] to write about because of the similarities between the author and me. We have very much in common: our politics, education, language, religious and cultural perspectives follow the same main stream, but radicating at different points. Thus not like Ricardo, I have spoken fluent Spanish all my life. Born in the U.S. and raised in a different country from the age of 6–14, I will specify that mine was not so much a problem of the English tongue as it was culture. As I read through this book, my eyes were fixed to every word and analyzed every sentence. In this paper, I will briefly quote Ricardo R. in several passages, to express my experiences and opinion to illustrate the likeness between us [1991, p. 25].

Belliard's essay is devoted to the many experiences and opinions he shares with Rodriguez, but it is dedicated to the finer distinctions and greater unities that give language its purpose.

Fumie Katsu, a Japanese exchange student spending her first term in the United States, effectively extends Belliard's notions of identification and purpose to her own emerging and all-important sense of audience. For Katsu, however, the initial bridge across difference is a longer one. In the prologue to her oeuvre ("Here Am I") she recalls her encounter with David Leavitt's *Lost Language of Cranes* (1986):

> When I started to write the third essay about [*Lost Language of Cranes*], I faced a difficulty with writing. The story . . . was about homosexual people. The main reason why I selected that story was that I was very interested in their way of life. I thought that their life was totally different from mine. But that story was about a family, which was not different from a normal family.
>
> I could involve myself very much with the main character and was very impressed. I really wanted other people to read that story. I tried to make my essay give the reader a strong impact. That was my first time to be conscious with the reader [1991, p. 1].

Belliard and Katsu discovered, quite on their own, through a process of reaching out in identification and rounding back in self-reflection, the key to effective writing: having something to say, and someone to whom to say it. Each demonstrates, too, the dual energizers of writing: the motivating force of self-expression and the more often overlooked draw of a receptive audience, present or imagined. These two located the writers in themselves; some students form a different sort of identity, locating the writer in their subjects.

Inessa Blanton's introduction to her oeuvre considers the formative influence of a writer's culture, as she describes herself, an immigrant to the United States just months before, in the third person:

> Inessa Blanton was born in 1965 in the Soviet Union. Being affected by the everyday dual existence of the majority of the population, she tryed to preserve her inner emotions and thoughts. Brought up on the ground of Russian classics, in her writing Inessa reflects those traditions. She is trying to understand hidden motives of the behavior of her heroes, to define the development of the characters [1991, p. 1].

Blanton's Reading Project essay, "Reading *Anne Frank: The Diary of a Young Girl*," for which she won a Writing Program award, continues those traditions, as she explores Frank's (1990) emerging potential as a writer and her tragic loss to world literature. At the center of the victim's diary, Blanton concludes, exists an inextinguishable writer's soul:

> This girl, had she lived, would have become a talented writer. She exhibited an insight into human nature—including her own—so fault-less that it would be surprising even in an adult. I would say that the main value of the book is that it was written by an unaffected young girl, exceedingly alive, deep, and honest. Here, in the Diary, her person-ality is on paper; it reveals the complete human being behind the pen [1991, p. 13].

Honesty, depth, and vitality are characteristics most of us do value in writers and their writing. Those of us who teach Basic Writing at the University of Massachusetts, Amherst, generally believe that these charac-teristics indeed must be valued, if our students are ever to develop the skills to complement them. We leave it to Esther Wung, eighteen months in the United States from Taiwan, to explain why in her oeuvre, "Writing is like composing a song by words. Reading is like listening to a song by eyes."

> I strongly feel that my writings are getting better since I got into this class. This is really a great class for those who really want to write something. . . . It is a big encouragement, writing in my own way and expressing whatever fantasy I feel. Every time when I get into "Fanta-sia," I let my mind imagine and all the fantasized things come out. That is extraordinary. Holding my pen, the words flow out like water flowing in the river, so gentle and so smooth. After I leave "Fantasia," there is

a paper finished. It is a great experience. And I think in [Basic Writing] I bring my ability in writing into full play. There is only one thing I want to say after taking this course for so long. "Writing is fabulous" [1991, pp. 2–3].

A Final Note

Wung is indeed right: "Writing is fabulous," richer and more fabulous than many of us believed before we entered on our new project. Perhaps it is we as teachers who have learned the most from our curriculum and from our students' progress through it; we who have experienced most acutely the disorientation of its culture shock and the equal exhilaration of new knowledge gained. The simple task of moving outside the familiar canon to search for unknown writings by seldom-taught writers at first struck us as daunting. The disempowerment we felt convinced us of the fundamentally political nature of our act. We were attempting to pull ourselves up by our own bootstraps. As teachers, we were attempting to create a curriculum out of material we had not been taught as students. And we saw that however progressive, even radical, we sometimes imagine education to be, it is, in fact, largely regressive. In other words, we were prepared to teach our students what our instructors had been prepared to teach us; we were well prepared, in short, to repeat the past and ill prepared for the present. Moreover, the past we were ready to teach was narrow, even distorted: what we ourselves had learned as "world" literature was really Western; "Western" was really Anglo American; "American" was North American, and Anglo North American at that. Now we feel that we teach the present through a curriculum that represents America as it truly is, one culture of rich texture and hue, constituted by myriad worlds that we, alongside our students, set out to explore anew each term.

References

Barthelme, D. "The School." *The New Yorker,* June 17, 1974, p. 28.

Bartholomae, D. "Inventing the University." *Journal of Basic Writing,* 1986, 5 (1), 4–23.

Bartholomae, D., and Petrosky, A. *Facts, Artifacts, and Counterfacts: Theory and Method for a Reading and Writing Course.* Upper Montclair, N.J.: Boynton/Cook, 1986.

Beaty, J., and Hunter, J. P. (eds.). *New Worlds of Literature.* New York: W. W. Norton, 1989.

Belanoff, P. "The Generalized Other and Me: Working Women's Language and the Academy." *PRE/TEXT: A Journal of Rhetorical Theory,* 1990, 11 (1, 2), 59–74.

Belliard, José. Untitled oeuvre. Unpublished manuscript, Freshman Writing Program, University of Massachusetts, Amherst, 1991.

Blanton, Inessa. "English 111." Unpublished manuscript, Freshman Writing Program, University of Massachusetts, Amherst, 1991.

Bleich, D. *The Double Perspective: Language, Literacy, and Social Practice.* New York: Oxford University Press, 1988.

Brodkey, L. *Academic Writing as Social Practice.* Philadelphia: Temple University Press, 1987.

Doctorow, E. L. *Ragtime*. New York: Bantam Books, 1976.

Dorris, M. *A Yellow Raft in Blue Water*. New York: Warner, 1988.

Elbow, P. "Reflections on Academic Discourse: How It Relates to Freshmen and Colleagues." *College English*, 1991, *53* (2), 135–155.

Fox, T. "Basic Writing as Cultural Conflict." *Journal of Education*, 1990, *172* (1), 65–83.

Frank, A. *Diary of a Young Girl*. New York: Pocket Books, 1990.

Gillespie, S., and Singleton, R. (eds.). *Across Cultures: A Reader for Writers*. Needham Heights, Mass.: Allyn & Bacon, 1991.

Harris, J. "The Idea of Community in the Study of Writing." *College Composition and Communication*, 1989, *40* (1), 11–22.

Henning, B. "The World Was Stone Cold: Basic Writing in an Urban University." *College English*, 1991, *53* (6), 674–685.

Hirschberg, S. (ed.). *One World, Many Cultures*. New York: Macmillan, 1992.

Hughes, L. "Theme for English B." In *Montage of a Dream Deferred*. New York: Henry Holt, 1951.

Hull, G., and Rose, M. " 'This Wooden Shack Place': The Logic of an Unconventional Reading." *College Composition and Communication*, 1990, *41* (3), 287–298.

Hull, G., Rose, M., Fraser, K. L., Castellano, M. "Remediation as Social Construct: Perspectives from an Analysis of Classroom Discourse." *College Composition and Communication*, 1991, *42* (3), 299–329.

Katsu, Fumie. "Here I Am." Unpublished manuscript, Freshman Writing Program, University of Massachusetts, Amherst, 1991.

Kingston, M. H. *China Men*. New York: Random House, 1989a.

Kingston, M. H. *The Woman Warrior: Memoirs of a Girlhood Among Ghosts*. New York: Random House, 1989b.

Lauter, Paul, and others. *The Heath Anthology of Literature*. Lexington, Mass.: Heath, 1990.

Layton, M. S. (ed.). *Intercultural Journeys Through Reading and Writing*. New York: HarperCollins, 1991.

Leavitt, D. *The Lost Language of Cranes*. New York: Bantam, 1986.

Paley, G. "The Loudest Voice." In *The Little Disturbances of Man*. New York: Viking Penguin, 1987.

Rico, B. R., and Mano, S. (eds.). *American Mosaic: Multicultural Readings in Context*. Boston: Houghton Mifflin, 1991.

Rodriguez, R. *Hunger of Memory: The Education of Richard Rodriguez*. Boston: Godine, 1982.

Roemer, M. G. "Which Reader's Response?" *College English*, 1987, *49* (8), 911–921.

Rose, M. "Remedial Writing Courses: A Critique and a Proposal." *College English*, 1983, *45* (2), 109–128.

Tan, A. *The Joy Luck Club*. New York: Ballantine, 1990.

Verburg, C. J. (ed.). *Ourselves Among Others: Cross-Cultural Readings for Writers*. New York: St. Martin's Press, 1988.

Walker, A. *In Love and Trouble*. Orlando, Fla.: Harcourt Brace Jovanovich: New York, 1973.

Walker, A. *Meridian*. Orlando, Fla.: Harcourt Brace Jovanovich, 1976.

Wideman, J. E. *Brothers and Keepers*. New York: Viking Press, 1984.

Wung, Esther. "Writing is Like Composing a Song by Words. Reading is Like Listening to a Song by Eyes." Unpublished manuscript, Freshman Writing Program, University of Massachusetts, Amherst, 1991.

MARCIA S. CURTIS is director, Basic Writing, and deputy director, Writing Program, at the University of Massachusetts, Amherst.

ANNE J. HERRINGTON is associate professor of English and director, Writing Program, at the University of Massachusetts, Amherst.

*Designing a course with curriculum content that addresses
both social diversity and social justice involves working with
multidisciplinary theories and perspectives, paying careful attention
to pedagogical issues, and creating an intentional community for
instructional support.*

Curricular Innovations: Social Diversity as Course Content

Maurianne Adams, Linda S. Marchesani

This chapter is written primarily for college teachers who share our efforts to combine cultural diversity with social justice subject matter in new undergraduate curricula. Examples of such courses are found within anthropology, psychology, and sociology, or among women's studies and ethnic studies offerings, and range from general education to major-specific courses (Tatum, 1992; Bohmer and Briggs, 1991; Hartung, 1991; Butler and Walter, 1991; Adams, Niss, and Suarez, 1991; "Curricular and Institutional Change," 1990; Williams, 1989). The course we will describe is a sophomore- or junior-level general survey, titled "Social Diversity in Education." It is offered across campus for majors and nonmajors by the School of Education within the context of a recently overhauled general education curriculum that requires all university students to select two courses meeting the "Social and Cultural Diversity" requirement from a broad menu of offerings. Our course addresses five subject areas: gender and sexism, race and racism, religious culture and anti-Semitism, sexual orientation and heterosexism, and physical or mental ability and ableism. Students are introduced to these five course subjects one at a time, in two-week segments, over a fourteen-week semester, as

We gratefully acknowledge the special contributions to the development of this course made by Sally Jean Majewski, Donna Bourassa, and several generations of instructors and graduate teaching assistants from the Social Issues Training Project, School of Education, and the Residential Education (Housing Services) teaching staff at the University of Massachusetts, Amherst.

conceptual linkages, parallels, and interconnections are incrementally drawn among them.

In this chapter we will first call attention to the foundational assumptions that govern the course, outline and provide examples of some realistic (in our experience) learning goals, and attempt through illustrations to convey a flavor of teaching strategies tied to learning goals and directed to the students we actually teach. We will briefly take up the general question of classroom to real-world learning transfer and conclude with some general principles of practice.

Foundational Assumptions That Govern the Course

First and most obvious among our governing assumptions is the interaction of social diversity with social justice as the conceptual base for the curriculum. In other words, students learn not only to recognize and appreciate social and cultural differences among the five areas noted above (for example, gender or race), but also to see those differences in the context of persistent societal oppression (such as sexism or racism). Students are encouraged to recognize and appreciate differences, but they are also helped to see the workings of a social system in which all differences are by no means equally respected. That is to say, an examination of cultural differences within specific contexts of historical and societal oppression leads one beyond simple "appreciation of diversity" to a perception of social inequities based on group dominance, social power, and privilege (Jackson and Hardiman, 1988; Blauner, 1972).

A second set of assumptions concerns the two intellectual traditions that inform both the curriculum and the pedagogy, namely, multiple disciplinary methods of inquiry and experiential learning theory. We utilize and combine theoretical perspectives and methods of inquiry primarily from the social and behavioral sciences, with special emphasis on developmental and social psychology and sociology, as well as from anthropology, history, and area studies (African American studies, women's studies, Judaic studies). This multiple disciplinary approach to course content is joined, however, to an educational approach rooted in experiential learning theory and active teaching strategies that pay attention to social relations within the classroom, the role of the instructor and a safe, respectful, confidential, and comfortable classroom climate.

A third assumption pertains to the background characteristics and prior experiences of our students. For the most part, whether from mainstream or underrepresented social groups, they come from more or less monocultural home and school communities that have not prepared them for the diverse populations they encounter on campus, the multicultural course content of some of their classes, and the range of cultural programs in the residence halls and elsewhere. Whether they are themselves from dominant or targeted social groups, the receptivity to and acceptance of other cultures and respect for social differences that are expected on campus may not have been practiced or valued in their home neighborhoods or among their peers and may even contradict the assumptions and beliefs of their families or religious backgrounds.

Our fourth and final assumption has to do with the necessity of ongoing instructional support and development for the teaching staff. A clearly delineated set of assumptions and learning goals in the curriculum does not translate swiftly and easily into specific teaching strategies. Instead, we find that each new semester's group of students and instructors bring new teaching and learning challenges into the classroom. Each year we work with a new group of instructors, helping them anticipate and deal with weekly classroom issues as part of a community of teachers who join together every semester for intentional instructional support.

Realistic Learning Goals

We cannot emphasize strongly enough that the learning goals for the course have become more modest and pragmatic with time, as our appraisal of the students becomes increasingly realistic. The goals include awareness, knowledge, and interpersonal skills as competencies we believe students will need for the multicultural world in which they are preparing to live, work, and build new families, schools, and communities. The goals are identified in the syllabus in the following ways:

Raising awareness: "develop an awareness of one's social identities, and your own and each other's social group memberships"

Information sharing: "establish a knowledge base about the dynamics and selected manifestations of social oppression, sufficient to allow for continued future learning"

Conceptual understanding: "apply methods of critical analysis drawn from psychology and sociology to an examination of the socialization process and of the systemic maintenance of oppression"

Recognition of real-world examples: "link new concepts and perspectives to observation and experience"

Intervention skills: "identify and practice new ways in which students can intervene on their own behalf and serve as allies for members of targetted social groups."

Raising Awareness. By this we mean identifying various categories of social identity (such as race, gender, and sexual orientation) and exploring the experiences among the range of dominant and targeted social groups represented within each category (for example, men and women, heterosexual and gay, lesbian or bisexual), with an emphasis on how these differences are regarded in the mainstream culture as well as in the university and classroom. "Awareness" or "literacy" about the complexities of cultural difference and societal oppression is not a given when students enter our class, but emerges as a gradual realization and remains the single most critical indicator of success with the course content. This increased awareness is related less to academic knowledge than to changes in attitude, receptivity, sensitivity, and openness to others. For example, dominant or mainstream students, in whatever area they may be dominant (by race or ethnicity, sexual orientation, or religion) tend to enter the class thinking of "difference" as the cultural "other," relatively oblivious to their own role as culture-bearers, and denying or downplaying the experiences of students who are socially subordinate or targeted. Thus male students (whether of European, African, or Latino heritage) may wonder what the "big deal" is for women who experience sexual harassment or are victims of acquaintance rape; until recent events in Bensonhurst or Howard Beach or Los Angeles riveted their attention, European-heritage students thought African- and Latino-heritage students exaggerated physical threats to their well-being or their perception of police intimidation.

Awareness is most readily achieved, in our experience, when the examples are accessible to students in their campus environments and recognizable in their daily interactions. By limiting the course to the areas of social identity most identifiable (if not necessarily most visible) to undergraduates in their college communities, we join personal and local data to the more abstract historical or sociological information. Admittedly each of these course topics, taken alone, could well amount to far more than a semester's agenda. The interconnections and insights that emerge among them, however, can lead to a deepened and more complex understanding of each issue. The student's awareness of his or her own social group memberships in relation to others in different social groups develops gradually across many weeks of observing, listening to, reading and thinking about, and discussing the experiences of members of different social and cultural groups.

Information. Here we are referring to individual, institutional, and societal instances or manifestations of prejudice and social oppression covered in this course. We draw our information from multiple sources including personal narratives, historical documents, and statistical figures. The information is presented via assigned readings, lectures, films, peer panels or guest speakers, or in-class shared experiences. This information is used to provide historical context and to reexamine prior misinformation, stereotypes, and prejudices; to fill in blanks caused by missing history or social invisibility; and to establish and model a pattern and expectation of lifelong inquiry and learning.

Although some of this information is personal—derived from individual stories and from local incidents of sexual or racial or homophobic harassment—the context broadens to include, for example, gender stereotypes in the media; statistical data concerning differential educational, income, and employment opportunities for people of color and women; historical backgrounds of European anti-Semitism; as well as racial laws and exclusionary quotas barring various racial and ethnic groups in this country's history.

Conceptual Understanding. The chief theoretical constructs and conceptual organizers that shape and integrate the knowledge base in this course offer the students a connection across the five subject areas. These overall constructs and organizers, drawn as noted from several social and behavioral science literatures, include (1) the process of social role identity, acquisition, and learning (conceptualized as a "cycle of socialization"); (2) the characteristics of social identity and social group membership; (3) the relationship between dominance and subordination, or "agent" and "target" groups in relation to social privilege and power; and (4) the levels (conscious and unconscious) and types (personal, institutional, cultural) of societal oppression in several historical contexts. Other concepts—such as stereotyping, scapegoating, internalization or collusion, and allies—are introduced as they prove useful in naming and understanding complex intrapersonal processes and interpersonal interactions.

These major constructs are introduced gradually and incrementally, woven in and out of our discussions over fourteen weeks and across the five subject areas (for example, gender, race, sexual orientation). For example, the cycle of socialization is presented early, not only as a foundational concept but because of its usefulness in helping students to organize and make sense of their own social learning. The cycle of socialization is presented in the context of "gender," the first subject taken up, and one with respect to which instructors can anticipate relative ease and familiarity on the part of the students.

We consider the cycle of socialization a foundational concept in that it helps explain the inevitable process of social learning by which all people acquire, in innocence and good faith, much of their initial knowledge and misinformation about "differentness" as well as their beliefs about themselves and their stereotypes and prejudices about others. The concept of social learning helps students understand that they are not to blame for the distorted messages or misinformation they acquire from various social contexts (family, peers, schools, media), but that they are responsible—once the process of critical inquiry has begun—for maintaining the process of inquiry, seeking out and acting on more adequate information.

The conceptual structure of the course involves both a backward and forward recycling of major constructs across the five designated subject areas. The concept of social learning (the cycle of socialization), for example, is reintroduced for each of the other four course subjects. Similarly, the construct of oppression as distinct from diversity is introduced several weeks into the course as we take up race and racism, although with retrospective applicability to sexism. This pattern of forward and backward reference is repeated with each foundational concept. For example, a consideration of the historical context of systemic oppressions—introduced with reference to the extended history of anti-Semitism—provides multiple instances of the levels and types of anti-Semitism in nineteenth- and twentieth-century European laws, media, and bureaucracy. The historical dimension, although detailed in depth for the first time on the topic of anti-Semitism, also suggests ways in which each oppression in the United States can be reframed and understood historically: racism, for example, against the background of slavery and forced segregation for African Americans, the World War II internment camps for Japanese Americans, the extermination of entire villages and cultures of Native Americans by colonists and westward settlers. Our students soon catch on to our method and understand that most of the major constructs introduced early with reference to gender, race, or anti-Semitism will be described again in relation to at least one other subject.

Some unexpected aspects of personal awareness will at times surface in the consciousness of students, out of the multiple parallels and interconnections that emerge among the several topic areas. For example, across-issue linkages and interconnections emerge at the personal level for students who experience multiple oppressions (an African American lesbian, a hearing-impaired Jewish woman, students from mixed racial parentage) as well as for students who experience multiple privileges (a heterosexual white Christian woman, a gay white Christian man, a heterosexual white Jewish man). Students begin to understand how their several internally interconnected social group identities, whether dominant or targeted, have internally reinforcing effects (Reynolds and Pope, 1991). Personal awareness of internal interconnection among multiple social identities also enables us to bring to the surface the complex category of social and economic class as it cross-cuts gender and race, and as it factors into some of the racial and ethnic stereotypes within racism or anti-Semitism.

Recognition. Recognition as a learning goal anticipates that students will learn how to look at their immediate world differently, to recognize the features of individual prejudice as well as institutional or cultural discrimination (such as homophobic harassment in the residence halls or the baiting of mixed-race couples, exams scheduled on Jewish holidays, or public gatherings that do not take the needs of students with disabilities into consideration). Such recognition involves students' understanding the multiple factors involved in real-life experience (such as the compounding effects of alcohol) as well as opportunities to practice disentangling multiple factors.

Recognition appears to involve three factors or sets of skills. First is recognizing the "figure" of prior classroom insights (such as examples of stereotypes) in the "ground" of current everyday life (peers telling jokes based on stereotypes). Second, for dominant students especially, is giving up the belief that violence or harassment is normal—caused by or exaggerated by the victim—and imagining the ways that things might be different. Third, recognition involves disentangling the complex ingredients of daily events and not simplifying them into either/or dichotomies.

It is indeed a challenge to engage in critical thinking on difficult issues about which most people have strong feelings and prior loyalties. Once one has recognized the complex issues within any single event, there remains the multiple viewpoints and multiple agendas—the role of alcohol or competing team loyalties that complicated and obscured the racism in one campus brawl (Hurst, 1988; "Frontline," 1988), for example, or the mutual stereotyping internalized and at work among African American, Latino, and Asian American groups competing for scarce resources on college campuses or the city streets.

Intervention. Admittedly difficult, recognition as a learning goal can be practiced through attention and case-study assignments and discussions. But recognition also implies intervention if the cycle is to be broken—and effective intervention, which cannot occur without prior recognition of what has occurred—assumes accurate problem solving, strategy options, and interpersonal skills that can also be learned and practiced. This cluster of learning goals speaks to the student orientation toward real-world relevance while also providing the requisite problem-solving strategies, range of possible and appropriate intervention, and skill competence that lets students feel able to *do* (at least at the interpersonal level) as well as to *know*.

Once students have tested the applicability of classroom learnings by disentangling daily events in case study examples, they often want to identify and practice intervention strategies as well. They do this first by reflecting on their personal actions in actual situations ("What did you actually do? What other options occurred to you at the time?") and second by beginning to imagine other possible behavioral responses or proactive interventions ("What do you wish you had done? What alternatives occur to you now, on reflection? What obstacles or enablers make these alternatives seem either difficult or possible?"). They are then prepared to try out alternative scenarios by projecting into the future ("What might you do if . . . ? What obstacles or enablers would block or ease various courses of action?"). Students can in this way learn to identify and acknowledge the differing risk levels of various intervention scenarios as they develop peer support from within class to practice, affirm, and carry out creative and positive interpersonal or campus change strategies. They identify spheres of influence (such as close family; intimate relationships; friends or peers at work, school, or places of worship; student activities, student government, and student newspapers; residence halls and classrooms), while also acknowledging that the risk levels involved may often vary inversely with the degree of intimacy and personal attachment.

Transfer of Learning

Each of the stated learning goals—awareness, information, conceptual understanding, recognition, and intervention—assumes the transfer of learnings from classroom to community, practiced most explicitly in relation to recognition and intervention—not left to chance, but systematically learned in a two-way process (Perkins and Salomon, 1989). In one direction, examples used in lectures and discussion are often drawn from immediate experience (personal, local, campus) and then disentangled, with students acknowledging each other's perspectives in their understandings of events. This approach allows students to reexamine shared experiences from the multiple perspectives available from their peers and to reflect back on those aspects of their socialization that limit their own initial perspectives. In the other direction, homework journal assignments leading to reflective papers help students to practice their recognition skills by recording and analyzing real-life experiences.

These two processes—self-reflection to gain insight into one's own perspective, as contrasted with perspective sharing and small-group discussions, and peers' narratives of experience contrasted with other sources of course content—bring alternative viewpoints on events from the outside world into the classroom and thereby establish a range of shared real-time, real-world experiences and perspective exchange within the classroom. It has seemed to us that our moral commitment within an academic course to use knowledge to inform action sometimes requires more explanation to our faculty colleagues than to students, many of whom still naively expect a reasonably direct interconnection between theory and life, facts and events, classroom and community, awareness and action, especially in a course that takes up some of the most pressing social problems of these decades.

Our own view is that the relationship between concepts and perspectives in the classroom and real-world, real-time observation and experience on campus or in home communities acknowledges a legitimate and important academic goal of learning transfer. That is, we hope to transfer classroom learning to the context from which all theory and knowledge presented in the classroom was originally drawn—the social world. The transfer from classroom learning back to the social world further acknowledges a pragmatic as well as a moral dimension of teaching in our particular university context, namely, the land grant undergraduate teaching mission (the preparation of an informed citizenry) of a state university that has also become a research university.

Teaching Strategies and Other Considerations

We have identified the underlying curricular goals, illustrated the interplay of course concepts to subject areas and learning goals, and accounted for the connections of knowledge to action that taken together characterize this course. Insofar as this course exemplifies a respect for knowledge, reflection, recognition, and practice, it is a traditional academic course.

But it will also have become clear that this course is characterized as well by a wide range of pedagogical tools and an unusually active learning mode, with activities and assignments and teaching strategies chosen as appropriate to the accomplishment of our goals. It seems to us, as to others who have contributed to the multicultural curriculum and general education transformation literature, impossible to separate our teaching strategies from the students' learning objectives (Tatum, 1992; Butler and Walter, 1991; Gaff, 1991; "Curricular and Institutional Change," 1990; Chapter Five, this volume). So it is both proper and necessary in conclusion to turn our attention to several overarching pedagogical principles that guide our teaching practice.

We draw our pedagogical principles primarily from the experiential tradition of active learning, the intellectual origins of which can be found in Dewey (1938), Lewin (1938, 1948, 1951), Piaget and Inhelder (1958), and Piaget (1971), and from the techniques practiced and perfected in cross-cultural and interpersonal sensitivity training: active learning, use of personal experience and local events, simulation activities and discussions, and attention to affect, self-reflection and interpersonal skills.

Principles of Practice

PRINCIPLE 1. *Theory-based pedagogy, not trial and error*

By and large, we have differentiated two broad theory-based domains, or reference points, for most of our teaching practice. These include principles of instructional design and principles of student development. The principles of instructional design, in turn, derive from antibias and antioppression education, rooted in broader traditions of humanistic and affective education, and from principles of multicultural learning styles, rooted in the broader learning style literature.

Thus, more immediately, from Weinstein (1988) and Weinstein and Bell (n.d.) we draw on the principles of humanistic and affective education in which antibias and antioppression education has been constructed.

These principles provide a framework for, first, an analysis of the limitations on an individual's ability to develop fully in the context of societal oppression; second, an appreciation of the tenacity and strength of emotion that attach to intergroup biases and beliefs, and the care and attention required for effective antibias education; and third, a set of procedures for developing the skills necessary to effect personal and social change.

From Kolb (1984) and Anderson and Adams (1992) we draw on experiential learning theory and cultural learning styles for principles of design informed by students' orientation toward action or reflection, to concrete or abstract cognitive processes, and by a substantial and wide-ranging repertoire of strategies informed directly by both the cultural style and learning style literatures.

We use principles of student development to help us anticipate and understand students' response to and engagement with the subject matter. These principles also inform our design and delivery of the various learning activities. The social identity model proves especially helpful in understanding the various forms in which the anger, denial, or pain associated with the subject matter is likely to be manifested by our students and felt by ourselves (see Jackson and Hardiman, 1988; Chapter Two, this volume; Tatum, 1992). It also helps us remember that students in our classes are in different places of identity development within the same social groups (for example, the male and female students, the heterosexual and gay, lesbian and bisexual students) as well as across social groups, so that we may anticipate the challenges presented by the collision of strongly held worldviews.

Similarly, we have been helped by cognitive development theory (Perry, 1981; Belenky, Clinchy, Goldberger, and Tarule, 1986) to anticipate students' tendency to dichotomize complex questions, to reduce multiple perspectives to either/or choices, and to fail in their initial efforts to see relations between concrete examples of experience and broader theoretical principles. Further, the cognitive developmental literature helps account for students' difficulties in disengaging from inside their personal experiences sufficiently to reflect from a broader or from a different social perspective. Finally, we have drawn on psychosocial identity development theory (Pascarella and Terenzini, 1991; Moore, 1990; Rodgers, 1990) to appreciate students' often competing developmental needs, on the one hand, to establish an individual identity and more autonomous self and, on the other hand, to see the individual self also as a social group member implicated in the dynamics of systemic oppression. Students in dominant social groups especially tend to see themselves exclusively as "persons" while at the same time generically seeing members of targeted groups as "women" or "people of color," an internal contradiction that we attribute to competing social identity, psychosocial, and cognitive developmental agendas.

PRINCIPLE 2. *Careful and explicit attention to process*

We are convinced, after years of teaching this course to various student populations and in different formats, that students pay special attention to the means by which we achieve our ends or teaching objectives. By process we mean, for example, establishing explicit norms and behavioral ground rules for mutual respect, confidentiality, non-confrontation, honesty, careful listening, and speaking for oneself but not for others. These norms and ground rules are added to and referred to throughout the semester to maintain a climate of personal safety and mutual respect that models the attitudes we are trying to teach (Tatum, 1992; Cannon, 1990). This aspect of process is important because it acknowledges the fears and anxieties students and teachers understandably attach to strong feelings invoked by the subject matter (see Chapter Three, this volume).

By process we also mean "processing time," one of the major rules of thumb in the workshop training literature, by which the time spent in processing or examining the personal and social implications of a learning activity is generally twice as long as the time spent initially to conduct the learning activity. Processing further includes a careful progression from personal reflection to small and then larger group conversations, all the while utilizing carefully sequenced questions to structure reflection on what was observed or learned from a film, a panel discussion, or simulation. By process, to give a fourth instance, we also refer to the use of deliberate, intentional preparatory structures to set up or "stage" many of the learning activities: questions attached to weekly reading and homework assignments, specific journal assignments, questions to generate personal information in anticipation of the three assigned papers for the course. Finally, we mean our conscious use of the facilitator's personae as well as our own experiences as dominant or targeted group members, while emphasizing by word, demeanor, and deed the importance of mutual respect.

PRINCIPLE 3. *Differentiate grades and evaluation from feedback*

Long before the media attention to political correctness in the multicultural classroom, we differentiated the ungraded written feedback we give to students, to challenge their thinking or point up disparities and inconsistencies, from grading and evaluation tied to their complete accomplishment of specific assignments and structured guidelines for papers throughout the semester. Students enter our class not initially believing us when we say that there are no right answers in this course. For our part, we have confidence that students who do the coursework will examine their own prior beliefs and assumptions, increase their knowledge base, grapple with theory and conceptual interconnections, and recognize course concepts in real-world examples.

Therefore, grades and evaluation are tied to work accomplished—responding completely (not cursorily) to questions about assigned texts and other readings, preparation of homework assignments, and completion of in-class activities; three written papers, each of which follows a sequence of reflective questions or structured guidelines; a final essay exam, based on broad conceptual questions that test students' utilization of concepts and knowledge. We may disagree with, even dislike and disavow, some of our students' views, but course grades derive measurably from assignments assessed solely in terms of questions thoughtfully answered. Individual assignments are quantifiable, and the final grades reflect numerically the totality of work accomplished. This procedure is especially important, we believe, as the political correctness controversy continues to threaten the integrity of our dialogue-and-discussion teaching approach. The more dualistic among our students, still inhabiting the dichotomous worldview of right/wrong, true/false, good/evil, might perceive a trend toward "political correctness" if we did not rigorously separate teacher-to-student feedback from performance evaluation and grading.

PRINCIPLE 4. *Attention to our own needs as college teachers*

As instructors of this course, we have our own professional as well as personal needs. We are continuing students of a complex, often volatile set of topics; we are members of multiple dominant and targeted groups sometimes "triggered" or disturbed by our students' or one another's interactions; we are individuals deeply committed to the subject and to the teaching/learning enterprise; and we are professionals engaged in reflection, observation, and research. We have for these reasons established as a fourth principle of practice maintaining ourselves as a community of teachers and learners via biweekly instructors' meetings, the development and dissemination of an instructor's manual based on designs developed by instructors within the course, and the ongoing observation and feedback sessions provided by faculty to the graduate teaching assistants and to one another.

References

Adams, J. Q., Niss, J. F., and Suarez, C. (eds.). *Multicultural Education: Strategies for Implementation in Colleges and Universities.* Macomb, Ill.: Western Illinois University Foundation for the Illinois State Board of Higher Education, 1991.

Anderson, J., and Adams, M. "Acknowledging the Learning Styles of Diverse Student Populations: Implications for Instructional Design." In L.L.B. Border and N.V.N. Chism (eds.), *Teaching for Diversity.* New Directions for Teaching and Learning, no. 49. San Francisco: Jossey-Bass, 1992.

Belenky, M. G., Clinchy, B. M., Goldberger, N. R., and Tarule, J. M. *Women's Ways of Knowing: The Development of Self, Voice, and Mind.* New York: Basic Books, 1986.

Blauner, R. *Racial Oppression in America.* New York: HarperCollins, 1972.

Bohmer, S., and Briggs, J. L. "Teaching Privileged Students About Gender, Race, and Class Oppression." *Teaching Sociology,* 1991, *19* (2), 154–163.

Butler, J. E., and Walter, J. C. (eds.). *Transforming the Curriculum: Ethnic Studies and Women's Studies.* Albany: State University of New York Press, 1991.

Cannon, L. W. "Fostering Positive Race, Class, and Gender Dynamics in the Classroom." *Women's Studies Quarterly,* 1990, *18* (1, 2), 126–134.

"Curricular and Institutional Change." *Women's Studies Quarterly,* 1990, *18* (1, 2), 1990. Special issue.

Dewey, J. *Experience and Education.* New York: Macmillan, 1938.

"Frontline: Racism on College Campuses." Public Broadcasting System (WETA), May 10, 1988.

Gaff, J. G. *New Life for the College Curriculum: Assessing Achievements and Furthering Progress in the Reform of General Education.* San Francisco: Jossey-Bass, 1991.

Hartung, B. "Unstratifying Stratification: Teaching Race, Gender, and Class." *Teaching Sociology,* 1991, *19* (1), 66–69.

Hurst, F. A. *Report on University of Massachusetts Investigation.* Springfield: Massachusetts Commission Against Discrimination, 1988.

Jackson, J. W., and Hardiman, R. "Oppression: Conceptual and Developmental Analysis." In M. Adams and L. Marchesani (eds.), *Racial and Cultural Diversity, Curricular Content, and Classroom Dynamics: A Manual for College Teachers.* Amherst: University of Massachusetts, 1988.

Kolb, D. A. *Experiential Learning: Experience as the Source of Learning and Development.* Englewood Cliffs, N.J.: Prentice Hall, 1984.

Lewin, K. *The Conceptual Representation and the Measurement of Psychological Forces.* Durham, N.C.: Duke University Press, 1938.

Lewin, K. *Resolving Social Conflicts: Selected Papers on Group Dynamics (1935–1946)* (G. W. Lewin, ed.). New York: HarperCollins, 1948.

Lewin, K. *Field Theory in the Social Sciences.* New York: HarperCollins, 1951.

Moore, L. V. (ed.). *Evolving Theoretical Perspectives on Students.* New Directions for Student Services, no. 51. San Francisco: Jossey-Bass, 1990.

Pascarella, E. T., and Terenzini, P. T. *How College Affects Students: Findings and Insights from Twenty Years of Research.* San Francisco: Jossey-Bass, 1991.

Perry, W. G. "Cognitive and Ethical Growth: The Making of Meaning." In A. W. Chickering and Associates (eds.), *The Modern American College: Responding to the New Realities of Diverse Students and a Changing Society.* San Francisco: Jossey-Bass, 1981.

Perkins, D., and Salomon, G. "Are Cognitive Skills Context Bound?" *Educational Researcher,* 1989, *18* (1), 16–25.

Piaget, J. *Psychology and Epistemology.* New York: Penguin Books, 1971.

Piaget, J., and Inhelder, B. *The Growth of Logical Thinking from Childhood to Adolescence: An Essay on the Construction of Formal Operational Structures* (A. Parson and S. Milgram, trans.). New York: Basic Books, 1958.

Reynolds, A. L., and Pope, R. L. "The Complexities of Diversity: Exploring Multiple Oppressions." *Journal of Counseling & Development,* 1991, *70* (1), 174–180.

Rodgers, R. F. "Recent Theories and Research Underlying Student Development." In D. G. Creamer and Associates (eds.), *College Student Development Theory and Practice for the 1990s.* Alexandria, Va.: American College Personnel Association, 1990.

Tatum, B. D. "Talking About Race, Learning About Racism: The Application of Racial Identity Development Theory in the Classroom." *Harvard Educational Review,* 1992, *62* (1), 1–24.

Weinstein, G. "Design Elements for Intergroup Awareness Training." *Journal for Specialists in Group Work,* 1988, *13* (2), 96–103.

Weinstein, J., and Bell, L. *Anti-Oppression Education: Instructional Issues.* Unpublished manuscript, University of Massachusetts, Amherst, n.d.

Williams, C. S. "Teaching Anthropology: Cross-Cultural Processes for Negotiating Meaning." *Urban Anthropology*, 1989, *18* (1), 85–93.

MAURIANNE ADAMS is a faculty member in the Social Justice Education Program and the Human Development Program, School of Education, and associate director of Residential Academic Programs, University of Massachusetts, Amherst.

LINDA S. MARCHESANI is assistant director of Residential Academic Programs and adjunct faculty in the Social Justice Education Program, School of Education, University of Massachusetts, Amherst.

PART THREE

Social Diversity on College Campuses

Three public universities had similar experiences as they grappled with the tasks of curriculum change, faculty development, "change agent groups," and assuring safe, supportive, multicultural campus climates.

Monoculturalism to Multiculturalism: Lessons from Three Public Universities

John A. Hunt, Lee Anne Bell, William Wei, Grant Ingle

The three campuses described in this chapter illustrate the problems and possibilities in moving from a predominantly monocultural to an increasingly multicultural campus. This essay analyzes the process of change on three campuses, identifies key issues common to all three, and draws lessons that may be helpful to other campuses engaged in this process. The three institutions—located in the Northeast and the Midwest—are simply called New England, Upstate, and Rocky Mountain, to focus attention on the common issues faced and lessons learned.

Like campuses throughout the country since the early 1970s, these three public universities have responded to pressures to increase numbers of students and faculty from previously marginalized groups, to develop equal opportunity and other campus programs to support these students, and to generate programs and courses in black studies and in women's studies. Such changes, although significant, generally operated separately from the rest of the university, thus leaving traditional practices, policies, and procedures unchanged. These public institutions, historically rooted in the land grant tradition of universal access to higher education at public expense, had combined a research-service mission with a teaching mission based on cultural assumptions shared by essentially European American students and teachers.

As admission of students of color increased, all three institutions experienced racial tensions and incidents that were not restricted to conflicts between whites and students of color. Sexual harassment, "gay-bashing," and anti-Semitic incidents mirrored conflicts in the larger culture and brought into question the notion that universities are ivory towers separate from the social realities that surround them (Dalton, 1991; Hively, 1990; Boyer, 1990). Students and faculty committed to combating racism and sexism and to inclusive admissions policies began to feel that "fixes" were finally of dubious value. What seemed required was transformation of the institution as a whole.

The right to pursue an education in peace and safety also had to be actively protected and affirmed. Simply recruiting more students and appointing token faculty or administrators from targeted social groups, without accompanying changes on the part of dominant group members and the institution as a whole, was a recipe for disaster. Changes in proportions of students implied changes in the institution, including curriculum, support services, student and faculty orientation, and teaching.

Intrinsic Impediments to Change in Academic Institutions

Before proceeding to specific case studies of institutional change strategies developed by the three state university campuses, it is useful first to consider some of the intrinsic impediments to change that appear to characterize academic institutions generally. These impediments are presented along with intervention steps actually taken at these institutions, or specific lessons learned.

High Student Turnover, Low Faculty/Staff Turnover. The failure to communicate new norms and behaviors appropriate to multicultural public institutions constitutes one obstacle to maintaining a safe and supportive campus. Typically, about 30 percent of the student population in public universities is new each year; the turnover in residence halls can be closer to 40 percent. Reaching this vast number of new students at the beginning of every school year (for some, at midyear) with important and complex social messages as well as factual information about university life is an issue that requires far more attention and analysis.

Faculty and staff also experience turnover, though at a much slower rate. However, although the problem is less urgent than with the annual (or semiannual) influx of new students, the need is equally serious for ongoing faculty orientation and staff-training, particularly about the changing nature of the student population.

Characteristics of New Students. Students of both the dominant culture and underrepresented groups often come to an unfamiliar campus culture from relatively monocultural home and school environments that leave them unprepared for multicultural norms and experiences. Worse, they may come from environments in which racial and ethnic conflict, sexual harassment, and homophobia are prevalent and more or less unchallenged facts of life. Combine these factors with susceptibility to peer pressure, inclination to abuse alcohol, stress from academic competition, higher costs, and a tendency among white students to believe that students of color get special privileges, and you have a prescription for conflict. For example, studies at the New England campus indicate that most incidents of racial harassment involve the combination of first-year students, alcohol, and friends from home visiting for the weekend. There is also a level of white backlash on many campuses manifested in such things as the call for "white student unions," drive-by verbal harassment and abuse, student publications that manipulate First Amendment rights to free speech in order to publish inflammatory matter that promotes racism, anti-Semitism, and homophobia (Dalton, 1991; Hively, 1990). Students from targeted social groups report instances of bias in police or administrative behavior. Thus it is not surprising that students from racially and culturally underrepresented groups band together for social support and political empowerment. The level of cohesion among students from targeted groups appears to have as much to do with their academic success as anything else the institution might support (Dalton, 1991; Wright, 1987; Chapter Two, this volume).

It is of interest to note that although no self-respecting university would send a student to study in another country without some cross-cultural orientation, including cross-cultural indicators of respect or disrespect, we think nothing of throwing students directly into a socially diverse and complex campus culture without providing the necessary guidance, education, and support to help them understand and survive in that new culture.

Ignorance of Student Experience. One of the most difficult tasks for university administrators and faculty is to understand and empathize with the ways students experience the institution. Faculty and staff tend to see the institution from their own limited perspective as a collection of discrete functional increments—schools or colleges, academic or student affairs units, physical plant, bursar, dean of students. Students, by contrast, tend to experience the university as an undifferentiated whole. Positive campus interactions have some short-term effect, but so do negative communications about overdue bills, housing experiences, and encounters with clerical or janitorial staff. Students from targeted groups especially may feel that disrespectful treatment by staff or faculty is directed at them as a result of prejudice, even when the behavior characterizes treatment of students in general.

The disparity between values and information in mission statements, catalogues, printed material sent to prospective students, and speeches at orientation, and what students actually experience, can be wrenching and disorienting. The Civility Commission at the New England campus was startled to discover in hearings with students from a number of targeted groups (African, Asian, and Native American students; Latinos;

gay and lesbian students; Jewish students) that all felt deliberately deceived about the campus atmosphere, the academic experience, and services and facilities designed to assist them. The contrast between expectations and experience was so traumatic that one student "cried for a whole semester."

As the cumulative experience of students is better understood, we might question our tendency to evaluate only the easily quantified elements of university life—hours in class, credit hours generated, locks replaced, parking spaces—and favor instead more serious if less measurable matters such as campus climate or social and cultural group interactions, all of which contribute to success for all students, but especially for students from targeted social groups. Three things arose from these commission hearings: first, there had to be a device for swift access to the authorities for aggrieved groups not well acquainted with the makeup of the university; second, what is learned from such access must be acted on and groups must be aware of the nature of the response; third, faculty and staff must try continuously to bridge the gap between their own perception of campus life and that of students. What emerges is the need for a new attitude, as well as reliable instruments to provide qualitatively useful information about the reality of student experience, and mechanisms for responding swiftly and proactively.

Implications of Changing Local Demographics. Despite an overall reduction in applications from the academic year 1987–88 to September 1991, the New England campus has maintained a proportion of incoming students from underrepresented groups that mirrors their 12 percent share in the state population. The institution anticipates that the numbers can at least be maintained, particularly in view of Department of Labor statistics that suggest an increasing population of minorities in the country into the first decade of the next century (Gerald and Hussar, 1991). Recruitment and admission of students from targeted social groups is a lesser problem than retention and graduation, issues that reflect the quality of academic preparation in secondary school and the nature of the experience at the university (Carter and Wilson, 1991; Smith, 1989; Wright, 1987). Our knowledge about underrepresented groups (and, as we have begun to realize, about most students) is insufficient in at least four areas: (1) the experience of socially targeted students in secondary schools; (2) their personal, social, and academic experience at the university; (3) campus supports appropriate to their needs; and (4) preparation that enables all students to communicate with one another knowledgeably and respectfully.

Governance and Administrative Complexity. For change at a university to occur, it is necessary for multiple governance units all to agree to new proposals. On most campuses, it is necessary for the chancellor or president, several of the vice chancellors or vice presidents, the faculty senate, faculty, administrative staff and their union(s), and student government all to agree if major changes are to become effective and institutionalized. Academic administrative structures, with their departmental territoriality, vertical lines of authority, and loose coupling among subsystems, are not well suited to establishing policy or responding rapidly to racial or other conflicts. Invariably, useful responses require horizontal collaboration across vertical lines of authority. Typically, embarrassing and well-publicized incidents result in the appointment of an ad hoc committee to investigate and recommend policy changes or other responses. Often recommendations for change do not fall obviously into any existing administrative jurisdiction and may be lost, leading to the perception (or the reality) of stonewalling. Horizontal interdepartmental communication links are needed at all levels, as are positive "institutional memory" devices to ensure that policy or process changes developed by recommending bodies are not forgotten.

Experience in the Residence Halls. There is little doubt that residence halls constitute for students the primary initial experience of a campus, and there is also little doubt that here, even more than in the classroom, there are opportunities for harassment and abuse, especially for students of color, women, and gays, lesbians, and bisexuals. One long-term intervention at the New England campus has been to sponsor continuing orientation and training for student residence hall staff, with special attention to the issues between and among students from targeted and dominant social groups. Training takes place in both orientation and course settings, which intentionally weave issues of race and ethnicity, gender, and sexual orientation into an understanding of multicultural community development, inclusive social and educational programming, and cross-cultural peer communication. Professional and student staff present the mainstream norms and values as belonging to one cultural tradition among many, not the dominant one against which others appear different or deficient.

Similarly, a Residential Academic Program brings into the residence halls sections of courses on social and cultural diversity which fulfill the general education requirement. These residentially located diversity courses attempt to develop a new college culture based on mutual understanding and respect bridged by shared academic interests and living/learning experience. These courses reflect the long-term collaboration of faculty from the School of Education and other academic departments who have experimented with various antibias classes and workshops dedicated to cross-cultural learning and intergroup respect. Programs in the residence halls bring together students from diverse social groups who share academic talents and interests, language or culture, and other areas of common learning; shared intellectual or cultural interests help forge positive residence hall experiences.

Achieving a Civil Campus Climate. The Civility Commission at the New England campus illustrates a response to an intrinsic difficulty for a multicultural university campus—the need to create a safe and supportive campus climate despite the repeated and escalating harassment and abuse among groups noted already in this chapter. The commission was established by the chancellor in 1980 in response to faculty and student demands that the university address increasing incidents of racism, anti-Semitism, and sexual violence; it was charged with investigating these problems and advising him about appropriate responses (Dethier, 1984; Ingle, 1991). Initial advice of this diverse group of faculty and staff resulted in the establishment of a broadly representative Civility Commission, with an Office of Human Relations as its administrative arm, to define and lead institutional change efforts, a year-long campuswide educational effort, and curricular change leading to the inclusion of two required diversity courses in the undergraduate general education curriculum. Later initiatives led to the development of a policy on sexual harassment (a process that, because of the governance and administrative complexities noted above, took five years to approve and implement) and a range of other policy and educational initiatives aimed at an improved campus climate and a more precise and effective response to issues and incidents.

The Civility Commission and the Office of Human Relations are especially significant because both report directly to the chancellor, avoiding the common tendency for these issues to be restricted and delegated solely to student affairs staff. The commission continues to advise the chancellor regularly, and the Office of Human Relations ensures adequate follow-through when recommendations are accepted for implementation. The result is a relatively coherent system for focusing administrative leadership on emergent issues in a way that provides continuity and accountability regarding efforts to create an increasingly multicultural campus.

The Office of Human Relations periodically sponsors public forums on the full range of human relations issues, including workplace conflict, and also convenes a biweekly meeting of senior staff from across all five divisions of the university to share human relations information, develop creative proactive responses before issues escalate to crises, and reflect on ways to improve future responses. The commission provides one approach to horizontal communication across vertical lines of authority.

The Process of Institutional Change

Most people who have attempted to enact significant change within academic settings could readily propose additions to this brief assessment of the chief impediments to change. Now we will move forward to describe several ingredients in the change process experienced by these three public universities, most notably their creation of institutional or curricular change agent groups, their support for curriculum change with consensus on clearly articulated curricular goals, and the centrality of faculty development programs to a successful broad-based curricular transformation process.

First, it is clear at all three campuses that the transition toward multiculturalism must be a high priority and a long-range goal within the basic mission of the institution (Green, 1989; Jackson and Holvino, 1986). The effort may be initiated by the top administration or by local programs reviewed through governance, but widespread support and commitment must be generated. At the Rocky Mountain campus in 1987–88, the campuswide strategic plan included "achiev[ing] a campus environment that supports and encourages gender, ethnic, and cultural diversity" (University of Colorado, 1988). In this way, a range of programs dealing with underrepresented racial groups became an integral part of the school's central educational mission, thus avoiding the tendency toward ghettoization of programs for underrepresented groups in a separate office of minority affairs.

A second consistent requirement is a broadly representative fact-finding, policy generating and implementing body with direct access to the highest campus officials. The Diversity Committee at Upstate, the Chancellor's Advisory Committee on Minority Affairs at Rocky Mountain, and the Civility Committee at New England were representative in membership of the social diversity as well as the institutional roles and departments of the campus. The Diversity Committee is more oriented toward the implementation of multiculturalism in the curriculum than the Chancellor's Advisory Committee or the Civility Commission, both of which are asked more for leadership regarding the total climate of the campus. At Rocky Mountain, for example, the Chancellor's Advisory Committee serves as a sounding board for campus minority issues and heightens the appreciation of cultural values and diversity on campus by identifying and generating proposals to deal with recruitment and retention of socially diverse students and staff and establishing a more inclusive curriculum.

Creating a Curricular Change Agent Group. The process followed at the Upstate campus is worth describing in some detail since it treats the membership issue, interaction process, handling of faculty conflicts between internationally and ethnically oriented academic programs, and consensus about what a multicultural curriculum should enable a student to do. Since a change agent group should broadly represent the constituent groups of an institution, including racial, ethnic, and gender diversity (Roberts, Bell, and Salend, 1991; Steinau-Lester, 1989), the composition of the committee created at the Upstate campus to address cultural diversity in the curriculum was broadly representative of the faculty as well as diverse in terms of race and gender. Two students were on the committee, and additional student input came from a long interview with student leaders who discussed their experiences in courses and their recommendations for change. These student interviews played an important role in motivating those committee members who had initially felt no urgency to examine the curriculum, and provided important suggestions for change.

Facilitation and Conflict Resolution Skills. Early on, two different orientations to multiculturalism emerged on the Upstate campus's Diversity Committee: one was a global studies orientation, the other was an ethnic studies orientation. An understanding of how these two orientations developed historically at Upstate was key to their eventual reconciliation and to the model of change that was adopted by the faculty.

In the early 1950s, Upstate had internationalized its curriculum by developing courses, hiring new faculty, and establishing a resource center in the library. For a time, global studies courses and foreign language study were required of all undergraduates, and study-abroad programs were developed in many countries. In the mid-1970s, Upstate responded to demands for courses in black studies and women's studies by founding departments or programs in these two areas. However, these developments were accompanied by economic retrenchments throughout the faculty that undercut many of the existing global studies programs and courses.

This unfortunate history resulted in antagonism and hostility toward the newer programs and a split between proponents of global studies on the one hand and ethnic studies on the other. Until this history and the perspectives it generated were sorted out, the Diversity Committee was unable to move forward. The breakthrough came through conflict resolution in which each side listened carefully to what the other valued, recognized the many commonalities that existed, and came to appreciate the distinctive contribution of each orientation to a comprehensive approach to multicultural change. The facilitating role played by committee participants able to exercise active listening skills cannot be overemphasized. A faculty consultant from another college also played a key role in helping the committee to articulate a comprehensive model for cultural diversity and curriculum change and, hence, to draw on the strengths and resources of both orientations. This integration informed the definition of cultural diversity that was developed and the curriculum changes the committee recommended.

Reaching Consensus on Curricular Goals. Questions of student learning goals and outcomes to be achieved through proposed curricular and pedagogical practices focused discussion on overarching ideals rather than on competing approaches to these ideals. The resulting process of consensus building in turn reconciled many at first seemingly insurmountable differences and led to a definition based on student learning goals and outcomes to which every member of the group could eventually agree. A culturally diverse curriculum would enable students to (1) develop an understanding of the pluralistic nature of American society; (2) develop a global perspective by learning about cultures in many regions of the world, appreciating their differences and similarities, and understanding alternative models of social and political organization; (3) challenge ethnocentrism and develop a concern for social justice by learning to take the perspective of other groups, particularly historically marginalized groups; (4) participate actively as citizens in promoting a more just and harmonious U.S. culture; (5) interact respectfully and knowledgeably with men and women from many different backgrounds and cultures; (6) think critically and act responsibly about the issues that face the world community in a time of shrinking resources, rapid communication, and increasing interdependence.

Using the Definition to Evaluate Curriculum. This inclusive definition guided discussions of curriculum change at Upstate and led to requirements in both global studies and ethnic and women's studies, criteria for determining how courses fit each category, and suggestions for new course development throughout the curriculum. The discussion required careful attention to different views and opinions, very specific and clear definitions of terms, and attempts to reach consensus. The committee treated seriously concerns about academic freedom, different views about how learning occurs and what constitutes good teaching, and turf issues with regard to course enrollments and resource allocation.

Faculty Development. The Diversity Committee at Upstate further recognized that a curriculum with the student learning goals outlined above inevitably affects pedagogical practices and classroom climate. Such a curriculum requires faculty to become aware of new scholarship in their disciplines, to review the structure and content of courses, and to examine pedagogical methods to include the many different voices of students. Such change also requires strong institutional support for faculty development and innovation.

Through discussions it became clear that faculty development was essential to the kind of transformation of the curriculum that long-range commitment to diversity entails. Committee members examined how other institutions had addressed the issue and summarized these strategies in their report to the faculty. Strategies included a lecture series, reading groups, workshops, targeting specific courses or areas for change such as American history or first-year composition, retreats, release time for interdisciplinary course development across departments, teaching and learning centers, sensitivity training, and ongoing support groups. The committee recommended that a variety of faculty development approaches be taken so that individual faculty could plug in where they felt most comfortable. Specific recommendations included sponsoring a seminar series on curriculum transformation for faculty, providing release time for a group of faculty interested in writing grant proposals to fund more intensive faculty development, providing space and institutional support for a Teaching/Learning Center on campus, and establishing a one-course release-time slot to be rotated among different faculty members who intended to develop new courses to meet the diversity requirements.

Institutional Support for Faculty Development. Implicit in all recommendations about faculty development is the necessity for institutional support. All three campuses emphasized the importance of leadership from the administration, unions, and faculty senate as well as of building in reward mechanisms for cultural diversity efforts. All three tried out mechanisms to institutionalize collaborative, ongoing efforts by, among, and between the faculty and staff. Explicit recommendations at Upstate included integrating diversity into the reward structure by making it an integral part of merit, reappointment, promotion, and tenure decisions; creating release time for diversity activities; institutionalizing funding and awards for diversity efforts; and committing adequate library funds for updating new scholarship in all the disciplines.

The Upstate campus also recommended institutionalizing a Teaching/Learning Center that would provide in-class observation and consultation to faculty who want to improve pedagogical skills or change their curriculum. In a similar vein, the newly instituted Center for Teaching at the New England campus incorporates workshops on multicultural teaching and learning styles, social issues in the classroom, and related topics into its annual teaching assistant orientation and its workshops for Lilly [junior faculty] Fellows, while informal linkages among faculty and teaching assistants serve to ease the extra challenges experienced by new teaching assistants of color. The Civility Commission also seeks partnerships with the Center for Teaching and academic departments to formalize pedagogical as well as curricular conversations among faculty who teach the general education diversity courses.

The Colors of Colorado: A Faculty Development Effort. The "Colors of Colorado" was a pilot project, similar in intention to the Upstate faculty development program, and organized to integrate the new racial and ethnic scholarship into the broader curriculum and to mainstream ethnic studies within multicultural education. Since it can be assumed that most faculty lack the expertise and incentive to include this new scholarship in their courses, Colors of Colorado proposed to provide expertise through faculty seminars that combined independent faculty reading, course revision, and instructional development work with cross-disciplinary group discussions, workshops and presentations by expert consultants, and assistance with resources such as teaching units, bibliographies, lists of audiovisual media, and demonstration syllabi. The incentive came in the form of stimulation provided by group activities, the opportunities for assistance via resources and consultants, and a modest honorarium provided to faculty participants. Though the original proposal called for its eventual campus-wide institutionalization, the Colors of Colorado never went beyond the pilot stage. Among the reasons for its premature demise, perhaps the primary one was an atmosphere of criticism rather than the anticipated collegiality and assistance. Since most of the faculty who signed up for the seminar were probably sympathetic to issues and concerns of social and cultural diversity, the atmosphere of criticism seemed especially counterproductive.

Curriculum Changes at the Three Campuses

The three campuses illustrate different approaches to establishing a multiculturally inclusive curriculum. At the Rocky Mountain campus, students in the College of Arts and Sciences have a single requirement within the core curriculum, by which they select courses from two lists, the one dealing with multiculturalism (women, race, ethnicity, and gender) and the second with global studies (cultures other than those of Europe and the United States). The Arts and Sciences requirement, designed to increase the students' understanding of the world's diversity and U.S. pluralism, appears to sanction existing divisions among faculty who believe the diversity requirement should focus on gender and ethnic diversity within the United States and those who focus on distinctions between international and domestic cultures. That division parallels territorial conflicts elsewhere (see Chapter Five) and other means of compromise and resolution (see Chapter Six).

At the New England campus, two social diversity courses are required of students within the campuswide general education curriculum and are selected from an extensive menu. Informal discussions have begun at New England toward reexamining the criteria for courses satisfying the diversity requirement, possibly opening on that campus an issue that has surfaced more concretely at Rocky Mountain and has been resolved by the inclusive criteria developed at Upstate. All three campuses face the questions, What are the criteria or learning goals for genuinely "multicultural" courses? and What support will permit faculty to develop such new courses?

A lesson learned in the efforts of all three campuses is the importance of faculty leadership, combined with reliable institutional support and avoidance of the pitfalls of academic turf and resource allocation based on enrollments. Finally, it was the experience of all three institutions that the process of collaborative curricular revision could be energizing for some faculty who were accustomed typically to working alone.

All three institutions inaugurated curriculum change in the 1970s by the establishment of women's studies and African American studies. All three have established "special opportunity" faculty positions that enable academic departments to recruit faculty from underrepresented social groups even when the department might not otherwise be entitled to recruit.

Observations and Future Directions

The broad-based movement at these three public universities, first to provide *access* as a higher education aspiration of the sixties, then to the reformulation signified by *appreciation of diversity,* and finally, to *multiculturalism and social justice,* appear to us to involve several interlocking imperatives.

1. The notion of the melting pot must be replaced with one of cultural pluralism or reciprocal multiculturalism. The issue is no longer one of adapting groups to a preset monocultural standard, but of co-creating a new multicultural standard that includes the contributions of all groups.

2. The importance of cross-cultural fluency or literacy must be acknowledged as an educational and curricular competency in preparation for negotiating life in a multicultural and multiracial society.

3. Institutions must recognize the task called for in changing higher educational institutions to meet the different personal, social, and learning needs of all students within a diverse student body and the personal security requirements of students from targeted social groups. Needed is a new sophistication in institutional analysis that is sensitive to the actual experiences of all students and responsive to problems as they arise.

4. Opportunities must be provided for faculty to learn about the new scholarship on race, gender, and ethnicity in their disciplines and to incorporate this knowledge into their courses. Faculty also need the opportunity to develop cross-cultural fluency in their teaching and classroom interactions.

5. The principle must be affirmed that all members of an academic community are entitled to pursue their work free of intimidation or harassment. Campus police, residence life and administrative staff, faculty, and students must work to create a campus climate where differences are affirmed and valued and to provide mechanisms to address grievances swiftly and effectively.

6. Institutional mechanisms must be created that reward faculty and staff who participate in multicultural change efforts. Mission statement, reward structure, and visible ongoing support all are essential.

The shift toward a multicultural perspective amounts to a "paradigm shift" or change in worldview that holds forth the possibility of a culture to which many groups contribute and within which all experience social justice. This change in worldview involves relinquishing the assumption that there is a pyramid of cultures based on relative value with one's own at the top. The new worldview involves the recognition of a diversity of cultures, each with its own uniqueness to be understood and cherished, as well as a mutual responsibility to establish an equitable community for all members. On college campuses, this goal means special opportunities as well as special challenges to develop new mechanisms for campus community and campus discourse. We ask ourselves whether the presence of two factions of American academic life, the *adapters* and the *preservers*—the one affirming the need to address new conditions, the other seeking to prevent threats to the values and traditions of the university—does not lead inevitably to competition, reliance on power as well as reason, and outcomes with winners and losers. We suspect that the prevailing win/lose campus mindset on issues of cultural pluralism and multiculturalism leads invariably to fragmentation, distrust, and the self-perpetuating struggle for campus power and resources that so many of us have experienced. We have thus come to believe that a better understanding of multiculturalism as a goal can help us work through our inevitable conflicts so that we learn from them, listen to and learn from the experiences and realities of diverse groups of faculty and students, and imagine the possibility for reaching an entirely new understanding of community.

References

Boyer, E. L. *Campus Life: In Search of Community*. Princeton, N.J.: Carnegie Foundation for the Advancement of Teaching, 1990.

Carter, D. J., and Wilson, R. *Ninth Annual Status Report on Minorities in Higher Education*. Washington, D.C.: American Council on Education, 1991.

"The Chancellor's Advisory Committee on Minority Affairs." *Faculty Review on Equity and Excellence*, no. 2. Boulder: University of Colorado, 1988.

Dalton, J. C. (ed.). *Racism on Campus: Confronting Racial Bias Through Peer Interventions*. New Directions for Student Services, no. 56. San Francisco: Jossey-Bass, 1991.

Dethier, V. G. *A University in Search of Civility*. Amherst: Institute for Governmental Services, University of Massachusetts, 1984.

Gerald, D. E., and Hussar, W. J. *Projections of Education Statistics to 2002*. Washington, D.C.: National Center for Education Statistics, U.S. Department of Education, 1991. (NCES 91-490)

Green, M. F. (ed.). *Minorities on Campus: A Handbook for Enhancing Diversity*. Washington, D.C.: American Council on Education, 1989.

Hively, R. (ed.). *The Lurking Evil: Racial and Ethnic Conflict on the College Campus*. Washington, D.C.: American Association of State Colleges and Universities, 1990.

Ingle, G. "Placing the Valuing Differences Approach in a Campus Setting: Complexity and Challenge." In M. A. Smith and S. J. Johnson (eds.), *Valuing Differences in the Workplace*. Alexandria, Va.: American Society for Training and Development Press, 1991.

Jackson, B. W., and Holvino, E. "Working with Multicultural Organizations: Matching Theory and Practice." In M. R. Donleavy (ed.), *Conference Proceedings of the 1986 Organizational Conference.* New York: Organization Development Network, 1986.

Roberts, G. W., Bell, L. A., and Salend, S. J. "Negotiating Change for Multicultural Education: A Consultation Model." *Journal of Educational and Psychological Consultation,* 1991, 2 (4), 323–342.

Smith, D. G. *The Challenge of Diversity: Involvement or Alienation in the Academy?* ASHE-ERIC Higher Education Reports, no. 5. Washington, D.C.: Association for the Study of Higher Education, 1989.

Steinau-Lester, J. "The Multicultural Organizational Change Process." *Black Issues in Higher Education,* Feb. 15, 1989, p. 104.

University of Colorado. *Challenging the Summit: Strategic Plan, 1987–88.* Office of the Chancellor. Boulder: University of Colorado, 1988.

University of Colorado. "College of Arts and Sciences Degree Requirements." Boulder: University of Colorado, Spring 1991.

Wright, D. J. (ed.). *Responding to the Needs of Today's Minority Students.* New Directions for Student Services, no. 38. San Francisco: Jossey-Bass, 1987.

JOHN A. HUNT *is associate professor of English at the University of Massachusetts, Amherst, where he has cochaired the Civility Commission and served as associate provost for Special Programs.*

LEE ANNE BELL *is associate professor of education, SUNY, New Paltz, and was chair of the campus Diversity Committee.*

WILLIAM WEI *is associate professor of history and Asian American studies at the University of Colorado, Boulder, where he was the first chair of the Chancellor's Advisory Committee on Minority Affairs.*

GRANT INGLE *is director of the Office of Human Relations at the University of Massachusetts, Amherst.*

Perhaps more than any other educational institutions, community colleges are on the forefront of dealing with diversity issues. This chapter describes how two leading institutions approach their special needs.

Community College Contexts for Diversity: Miami-Dade Community College and Joliet Junior College

Mardee S. Jenrette, J. Q. Adams

In this chapter we will examine the approaches that two different community colleges have developed for dealing with issues of diversity. Although the colleges vary in size, location, demographics, and history, they share some commonalities that illuminate institutional change processes.

At first glance, however, it is the differences between the two community colleges pictured here that are most striking. One was established thirty years ago, at the height of the community college movement. The other, at ninety, is the oldest public community college in the country. One has a student body eight times the size of the other with four times the percentage of minority student enrollment. Study the two pictures carefully, however, and important similarities emerge—in the changes made toward better student assessment and placement, curriculum reform, faculty selection, and the overall institutional goals for each college—at the same time that the methods for soliciting input, the reward structures, and the monitoring processes reveal different approaches.

Both colleges have come to see the establishment of a diverse collegiate environment as essential to the provision of high-quality service to their communities. Both identify similar elements as keys to attaining that goal: attracting and retaining a diverse student body, attracting and retaining a diverse staff, broadening instructional repertoires, faculty and staff development to ensure successful implementation, and curriculum change as a vehicle to introduce diversity issues to students and staff. Both institutions have made a strong commitment to encouraging diversity and have been willing to invest considerable time, resources, and systematic institution-wide efforts to bring that commitment to reality.

Miami-Dade Community College

Miami-Dade is a multicampus, urban and suburban community college. It annually serves a credit student population of approximately 79,000 with a full-time staff of 2,500, of whom 900 are faculty. Dade County, the college's immediate community, has undergone considerable demographic shifts since Miami-Dade Community College first opened its doors in 1960. Principal among them has been an influx of Cuban refugees combining with other Latin Americans to increase the numbers of Hispanic residents. The county now boasts a total population of two million. Reflecting its community, the open doors of Miami-Dade Community College have brought an increasingly diverse and nontraditional student body into its classrooms in the last decade and a half. In addition to the Hispanic influence, the college is the primary higher education destination of the county's African American population and is serving increasing numbers of Haitian refugees as well. Miami-Dade attracts a larger number of foreign students annually than any other college or university in the United States. In 1992 the student profile was 55 percent Hispanic, 19 percent black, and 23 percent white non-Hispanic; over 50 percent are nonnative speakers of English; two-thirds enter academically deficient in at least one basic skill area; 75 percent qualify for financial aid; most juggle school, jobs, and family.

Change Brings Reform. During the late 1970s and early 1980s, Miami-Dade underwent a major reform initiated by president Robert McCabe and triggered by the challenges presented by its steadily diversifying student body. To provide nontraditional students a quality college education would require the institution to design and deliver special support services to enable them to take advantage of the academic programs offered. Under the banner of access with excellence the college strove to assure every student the opportunity to succeed. Processes were instituted that changed the way entering students are assessed, advised, placed, and later given feedback on their academic progress. Accompanying sweeping systemic changes were curricular ones that expanded developmental course work and produced an integrated general education program (Roueche and Baker, 1987).

At the same time the Miami-Dade student body was changing dramatically, the faculty had remained remarkably stable (twenty-one to twenty-five are the modal years of service). However, by the 1990s, many veteran faculty members would be reaching retirement age. The implications of significant staff turnover provided the impetus for the president, in late 1986, to propose a second major institutional initiative, the

Teaching/Learning Project. Through this reform the college would move toward several goals: diversification of the faculty, a restructuring of the reward system so that performance congruent with the missions and values of the institution would be appropriately recognized, adoption of a statement of excellence in the faculty role that would be based on qualities that enhance the learning potential for a diverse student body, the establishment of a support system to assist faculty striving for excellence. To be truly meaningful, the change in the college would have to be massive. What better time to institute sweeping change than when one-third to one-half of the faculty would be new?

An Institution-Wide Response to Meet Student Needs. By 1987 the college had embarked on what soon would be called the project that ate Miami-Dade because it left no segment of the institution untouched. When faculty and administrative leadership were asked, "What must we do to enhance teaching and learning at Miami-Dade to meet the needs of our new student body?" an intense examination of the teaching/learning relationship was launched. Every phase of the operation, from what was going on in the classroom to what was happening in the purchasing department, was scrutinized (McCabe and Jenrette, 1990).

Issue-based task forces of college faculty and administrators, coordinated by a project director and college-wide steering committee, investigated current college practices and then made recommendations of changes that should be made to accommodate the diverse needs of our student body. Support for teaching and learning activities and altering decision-making practices to give teaching and learning greater priority emerged as major focal points. Because time was taken to investigate carefully and get input, emerging recommendations were truly reflective of college needs. Once recommendations were made, providing the opportunity to reshape them after a broad-based feedback process, and adopting them only after approval from key faculty and administrative decision-making bodies, ensured substantial buy-in.

Five years after its inception, the Teaching/Learning Project has brought considerable change to the college: a system to monitor the classroom physical plant has been devised; offices for faculty have been built to new standards; centers for teaching and learning have been opened on each campus; a five-day preservice orientation and mentor program have been initiated for new faculty; two graduate courses in teaching and learning for new faculty have been developed; sixty teaching chairs have been endowed.

During the same five-year period the predicted faculty retirement increases also began. For the period of 1988–1991, eighty-one veterans left the institution. Of those, 93 percent were white non-Hispanic. Their replacements are 47 percent black and Hispanic.

While a number of threads can be found in the complex web that is the Teaching/Learning Project, a major one clearly deals with diversity: the increasing diversification of the student body, the concomitant diversification of the college's staff, the need to create a climate and culture supportive of diversity. Tracing that thread from rhetoric to reality and from principle to practice might provide useful information to others with similar missions, encountering similar conditions.

Foundation Based on Clear Values and a Definition of Excellence. One of the initial objectives was to provide a foundation on which the rest of the project could be built. Through an eight-month period of surveying students, faculty, staff, administrators, and community members, and through drafts, feedback, and redrafts, a task force struggled to articulate a single set of values that the Miami-Dade community could embrace. At the conclusion of the process, and having achieved college-wide consensus, in 1988 the district board of trustees adopted seven teaching/learning values and indicators by which the institution could demonstrate that it was acting consistently with those values.

Among the seven were these two that bear on diversity directly:

- Miami-Dade Community College values access while maintaining quality.
- Miami-Dade Community College values diversity in order to broaden understanding and learning.

A number of the value indicators proved to be more indicative of what the institution felt it should be doing than of what it really was doing at the time. Paper recognition served as a first step toward closing the gap between *should* and *does*. Strides have been made in the last few years to demonstrate Miami-Dade really does value diversity. To provide two illustrations from the perspective of personnel: a self-imposed policy makes 50 percent the target for minority professional and faculty hires; a minority fellowship program annually gives five recipients $10,000 each to complete a master's program in return for three years of full-time teaching in Miami-Dade classrooms with the intention of building a career-long relationship between the college and the individual.

Much discussion from the inception of the project focused on excellence in teaching as an essential ingredient in the enhancement of learning. It was clear, as well, that excellent performance would have to be nurtured and rewarded by the institution if Miami-Dade was truly to maintain its status as a premier teaching institution. If excellence were to be the focus, then its definition would have to be agreed on by those who would display it (faculty) and those who would support and reward it (administration).

Would it be possible to create a definition that would be focused and yet would accommodate the myriad individual styles and curricular needs that make teaching/learning relationships so challenging, dynamic, and personal? Would it be possible to encourage diversity yet at the same time reach agreement on a common core of qualities? For Miami-Dade the answer in each case was yes. The Miami-Dade Community College Statement of Faculty Excellence is a twenty-nine-item narrative that describes faculty qualities that facilitate student learning. Faculty, administrators, and students all contributed to and then validated these qualities during an eighteen-month adoption process that featured research, surveys, focus groups, retreats, drafts, feedback, and redrafts. The statement presents *what* an excellent faculty member does, but leaves the *how* to the individual. To provide a few examples, excellent faculty members at Miami-Dade Community College, whether classroom teachers, librarians, counselors, or serving in any other faculty capacity:

- Project a positive attitude about students' ability to learn
- Create a climate that is conducive to learning
- Are knowledgeable about how students learn
- Integrate current subject matter into their work
- Provide perspectives that include a respect for diverse views
- Provide students with alternative ways of learning.

The importance of a document of this type to an institution striving to accommodate a diverse staff and student body cannot be overstated. No longer will someone's "different" teaching style be considered unacceptable if it clearly addresses qualities that are among the twenty-nine and its positive effect on student learning can be demonstrated. No longer will it be assumed that there is one best approach to teaching that will enable all students to learn. Further, because the Statement of Faculty Excellence was reached by consensus, it is understood that these qualities are right for Miami-Dade.

Much can be accomplished from a common shared values base and definition of excellence. Potential faculty have a clearer impression of the institution and can determine their fit before pursuing application. The institution, on its side, can focus its assessment of candidates (beyond discipline-based concerns) more clearly on what it deems important. Institutional reward systems (tenure, rank promotion) can be aimed at what faculty want to be recognized for. Faculty development programs can be mainstreamed, in that they can be designed to provide faculty opportunities in areas that they themselves have identified as important for their work with Miami-Dade students (Weimer, 1990).

Rewarding Excellent Performance. Of great significance in promoting excellent performance is the formal reward system of an institution. At Miami-Dade the reward system has been incorporated into a set of policies and procedures called Faculty Advancement. Faculty Advancement includes tenure, promotion, and the awarding of endowed chairs. All components have at their heart a set of performance-based criteria derived from the Statement of Faculty Excellence. Two key strategies driving decision making within the Faculty Advancement system are a college-wide student feedback/classroom assessment program and the use of faculty-developed portfolios to document performance.

New faculty members are given three years before a committee of colleagues reviews their candidacy for tenure. During that period, with the statement as their guide, and working with mentors, they hone their skills. Part of the skill building includes completion of two graduate courses designed through the Teaching/Learning Project and taught by the University of Miami. One course focuses on assessing learning using classroom feedback and assessment techniques. During the term in which they are enrolled in the course, faculty have the opportunity to use their own classrooms as laboratories, trying out new techniques and immediately assessing the impact on student learning. The second course profiles the Miami-Dade student body, emphasizes differences among learners, and explores ways in which faculty can address diverse needs. At the end of the three-year probationary period, candidates present their teaching portfolios. A narrative and documentation coming from multiple sources (students, self, peers, department chair) provide evidence to the tenure committee that standards of excellence derived from the statement have been met.

Candidates for academic rank promotion and endowed teaching chairs go through essentially the same process as the tenure candidate: providing committees of peers clear evidence (through a portfolio) that they have met the standards of excellence required for the rank or reward they seek. Individuals who wish to participate in the college's formal reward system are expected, as they progress through their careers, to demonstrate an increasing number of the qualities of excellence and to share their expanding expertise with an ever-broadening audience.

Making Learning Everyone's Responsibility. Having excellence defined by those who must exhibit it, providing support and professional development opportunities to achieve it, and rewarding the achievers is proving so effective in helping faculty carry out their responsibilities that the development of similar procedures for administrators and support staff was initiated in 1990. Although the outcomes will certainly be shaped by the specific responsibilities of those two groups, the basic question to be addressed remains the same—What will it take to be able to contribute to an effective teaching/learning environment for our diverse student body? Also in the planning stages is an invitation to students to define for themselves a statement of excellence. The teaching/learning relationship cannot flourish without significant participation from both faculty and student partners.

The Teaching/Learning Project has an impact on all sectors of the college, making a reality of the concept that teaching and learning are everyone's responsibility. Individuals examine their own behavior and measure the services they provide against the teaching/learning yard-stick. The number of conversations occurring in the offices of faculty, administrators, and staff about what is good for students has increased dramatically. Rallying around a common mission has bridged gaps between faculty, administrators, support staff, and students.

Joliet Junior College

On November 17, 1991, Joliet Junior College (JJC), the nation's oldest public community college, celebrated its ninetieth anniversary. JJC started as an experiment in postsecondary education at Joliet Township High School (in Joliet, Illinois) in cooperation with the University of Chicago, to inspire academically able students from Joliet's working class to continue their educations after high school graduation. As a result, these students were able to attain the general educational skills that many college leaders at the time felt should be mastered before the specialization the university should provide. Thus this experiment became the pioneering model of the junior and community college movement across the nation (Wood, 1987). Beginning with six students in 1901, JJC now boasts a student enrollment that exceeds 10,000. Fifty-nine percent of the student body is female. The mean age is 25.4 years. The ethnic diversity is as follows: African American, 7.4 percent (746); Asian American, 1.3 percent (128); European American, 87.1 percent (8,755); Latino, 3.8 percent (384); Native American, .02 percent (19); and other, .01 percent (12).

Since its inception JJC has celebrated diversity, quality, and opportunity for the community it serves, which now has a population of over 400,000 in the 1,400-square-mile district that includes Will, Grundy, Kendall, Kankakee, LaSalle, Livingston, and Cook counties. This district is best characterized as a blend of rural farmland and agriculture-related businesses and the suburban sprawl from Chicago with its high-tech specialized economies.

Institutions such as colleges and universities seldom move toward diversity because it is the right thing to do; instead they change as a result of internal or external catalysts. JJC's move toward diversity was a result of both of these forces over a twenty-year period, beginning in the early 1970s. At that time the college hired its first black faculty members, one of whom would later become one of the first elected black community college trustees in the state of Illinois. In 1984 a second black trustee was elected. These events, along with the community and political activism of the period, formed the necessary critical mass for change that led to reinterpreting the mission and goals of the college. One example of the board of trustees' increased attention to diversity was the creation of the Office of Minority and Intercultural Affairs. The new director of this program developed and facilitated a variety of activities to foster multicultural education and cross-cultural understanding: the Joliet Area Math, Science, and Computer Education Enrichment Project, the Brown Bag Lecture Series, a minority student transfer program, World Food Day, and a cross-cultural concert series are some of these programs.

In 1985, a seasoned community college administrator from the Philadelphia community college system was hired as the new president and quickly assessed the college and community's needs, developing a master plan that included issues in diversity as one of its major goals. As a result of the board of trustees' increased sensitivity toward diversity issues and the equity and equality concerns of its new president, the slow process of change began to build momentum at JJC in visible, concrete ways. Some examples of these changes are summarized below.

Master Planning Process. During the spring of 1987, JJC's board of trustees approved a strategic planning initiative presented by the president's staff that involved the entire college community including faculty, staff, students, parents, and citizenry from the district. The president's staff took care in the selection of participants to insure representative diversity and input from across the district. In a series of town meetings, 119 issues and alternatives were identified as pertinent to the growth of the college, which led to the development of the college's master plan in 1988 (Joliet Junior College, 1989). Key administrators, under the direction of the president, analyzed, prioritized, and monitored the issues as they were assigned to staff, and by the winter of 1990, 92 percent of the high-priority issues were either completed or ongoing (Joliet Junior College, 1991). Some of the most significant results and successes directly bearing on the diversity of the student body included mandatory basic skills assessment, an automated learning resource center, a pilot student orientation course, and a full-time minority enrollment coordinator.

The college's master plan is not a static document but a living, breathing process that is still used to inform staff and community and help share the direction of JJC. In the fall of 1991 another town meeting was held with more than fifty volunteers from the community. The suggestions generated from those in attendance will be included in the college's master plan.

Range of Student Services. The Joliet Area Math, Science, and Computer Education Enrichment Project (JAMSCEEP) was developed in 1986 as the result of a grant through the Illinois State Board of Education. JAMSCEEP provides tutorial and mentoring opportunities for high-potential junior and senior high school students from Illinois Community College District 525. This program has successfully helped more than

231 ethnically diverse students. Ninety-two percent of the students who stayed in the program until high school graduation successfully enrolled in the postsecondary programs of their choice in colleges and universities within the state (including JJC) and across the nation.

Minority Enrollment Office. In order to understand and address the special needs of students from underrepresented social groups, JJC developed the Office of Minority Enrollment, which assists in its recruitment and retention efforts. These include working with the counselors at targeted high schools through the Minority Recruitment Program, which facilitates minority student visits to the college. This office also coordinates a five-day Reaffirming Academic Priorities program each semester for minority students currently enrolled at JJC. Students are helped to develop good study skills and strategies for overcoming test anxiety. The director of this office also acts as a liaison between JJC and the numerous community agencies and programs that serve the diverse populations in the district.

Transfer Center. This concept arises from a statewide project involving all fifty community college campuses in Illinois. The major goal of the project is to increase the minority transfer rate from the community colleges to the four-year colleges. Two hundred students were served during the fall of 1991, 30 percent from underrepresented groups.

Office of Student Services and Activities. This office functions like many service centers of a similar nature on college campuses. But unlike many others, it has a unique commitment to providing student experiences that foster a respect for cultural differences and diversity in general. In order to accomplish these goals, numerous programs have been established to provide students in general, and student leaders in particular, with the training necessary to work effectively in a multicultural environment. In one such program, student leaders participate in a weekend retreat during which cross-cultural communication training takes place.

Academic Programs, Curricular Change, and Faculty Development. JJC has developed, and is in the process of integrating, a variety of innovative approaches for fostering and teaching about diversity, including both multicultural and international options. New faculty hires are drawn from an international pool (India or Africa, for example) more frequently than from a domestic multicultural pool, and study-abroad options are European. Although both international and domestic multicultural studies ultimately foster similar cross-cultural and intercultural perspectives on mainstream American culture for students from the dominant groups, there is an undercurrent competition for resources between the two that resembles the conflicts over turf and perspectives notable on other campuses (see discussion in Chapter Four).

In addition to its academic programs JJC has also made strides in developing its vocational programs to meet the needs of a multicultural economy. An example of this is the college's Automotive Services Department, which was selected by Toyota Motor Sales, USA, to train students for the Toyota Technical Education Network (T-Ten).

In 1988 a faculty member developed and taught a course entitled "Cultural Diversity in America" for the first time. Three sections of the course are currently offered each semester with enrollments that exceed a hundred students per semester (Mattai, 1991). A curriculum infusion project funded through a U.S. Department of Education grant has focused primarily on international course content, but includes multicultural content as well, in courses such as children's literature, education, fashion industries, sociology (eco-housing, marriage and the family, social problems). Courses with international focus range from agriculture to business and from geography to microbiology.

Staff Development. JJC's staff development has played a crucial role in providing consistent focus and leadership in helping promote faculty and staff awareness of the importance of diversity issues in the workplace as well as in the classroom. The faculty development program that starts off each new semester regularly features several workshops on pluralism and social diversity as a consistent theme. Numerous programs are presented by guest speakers and workshop leaders for faculty and staff on key diversity issues such as cultural learning styles, international education, multicultural awareness, the older student, and cultural sensitivity. The annual Outstanding Employee awards are based in part on efforts to work with underrepresented students or to develop multicultural programs. Recipients are selected by a committee of peers, department chairs, and students for their outstanding contributions in the classroom, so that classroom responsiveness to diversity becomes part of the regular award structure.

Conclusion

An institution that decides to engage in a project of this nature makes a commitment of considerable time, expense, and probably some risk as the status quo is challenged. The experience at Miami-Dade Community College, after five years of its Teaching/Learning Project, and at Joliet Junior College, suggests some ways in which specific programs toward greater student and staff diversity can continue in the pioneering, innovative spirit that their founders displayed initially. Examples of community colleges that serve increasingly diverse student populations are of increasing importance as an avenue to postsecondary opportunities for a number of multicultural communities. If creative foresight, positive intrusiveness, and a commitment to the issues of equity and equality are to continue, greater emphasis must be placed on hiring and retaining a diverse, multicultural faculty at both institutions featured here. Miami-Dade has developed the Teaching/Learning Project with a number of innovative support and evaluation features toward that end. At Joliet, an effort that parallels the current emphasis on international education will be needed to provide a diversity in domestic faculty that reflects both the students it teaches and the global village in which they will eventually live and work.

References

Joliet Junior College. *Executive Report 1985–1989.* Joliet, Ill.: Joliet Junior College Office of Community Relations, 1989.

Joliet Junior College. *Master Planning: A Plan for Success, a Plan for the Future.* Joliet, Ill.: Joliet Junior College Office of Community Relations, 1991.

McCabe, R. H., and Jenrette, M. S. "Leadership in Action: A Campuswide Effort to Strengthen Teaching." In P. Seldin and Associates (eds.), *How Administrators Can Improve Teaching: Moving from Talk to Action in Higher Education.* San Francisco: Jossey-Bass, 1990.

Mattai, B. "Teaching About Cultural Diversity: Challenge and Response at a Community College." In J. Q. Adams, J. F. Niss, and C. Suarez (eds.), *Multicultural Education: Strategies for Implementation in Colleges and Universities.* Macomb: Western Illinois University Foundation, 1991.

Roueche, J. E., and Baker, G. A. *Access and Excellence: The Open-Door College.* Washington, D.C.: Community College Press, 1987.

Weimer, M. *Improving College Teaching: Strategies for Developing Instructional Effectiveness.* San Francisco: Jossey-Bass, 1990.

Wood, S. H. *The People's Legacy: A History of Joliet Junior College, 1901–1984.* Joliet, Ill.: Joliet Junior College Foundation, 1987.

MARDEE S. JENRETTE is director of the Teaching/Learning Project at Miami-Dade Community College.

J. Q. ADAMS is associate professor in the Department of Educational Foundations at Western Illinois University.

Two models for institutional transformation to educate a pluralistic student body illustrate the importance of a focused mission and a coherent curriculum made inclusive through faculty development.

Institutional Transformation for Multicultural Education: Bloomfield College and St. Norbert College

Martha J. LaBare, Stuart G. Lang

Small colleges have the opportunity to respond to diversity dramatically, perhaps more thoroughly and quickly than large institutions. Yet they share with larger, more complex institutions several change strategies essential to success. These include philosophical commitment to access and equity, strong leadership, effective communication among and involvement of all constituencies, coherent and flexible planning, and funding—both by the reassignment of institutional budget and from new resources.

Bloomfield College (New Jersey) and St. Norbert College (Wisconsin) are both small, church-related, coeducational, liberal arts colleges. Both are committed to diversity, although working from different histories and with different student populations. Bloomfield's students come primarily from urban areas in New Jersey; roughly half are adults returning to college. Half are African American or Latino. The majority of St. Norbert students come from suburban or rural homes in Wisconsin and northern Illinois, and 95 percent are full-time, traditional-age white students. St. Norbert seeks to add diversity to a predominantly European-heritage student clientele; Bloomfield seeks to build community from an already diverse student body.

In spite of these differences, the paths both schools are following to promote change and to achieve support for diversity show strong similarities. As part of their overall institutional change, both colleges have sought to broaden their curricula: St. Norbert first with a degree and certification program for a specific Native American population, Bloomfield with a college-wide program for faculty development and for inclusive curriculum, academic support, and student development. Similarly, change at both colleges has been led by their presidents and key faculty and supported by new grant moneys. Both colleges (though at different stages of the process) illustrate the institutionalizing of changes within the faculty, staff, and budget commitments.

These two snapshots illustrate procedures for establishing faculty commitment and curricular change as well as the involvement of all constituencies in a collegiate plan.

Bloomfield College

Bloomfield College's "Excellence Initiative" was established to implement the college's mission to prepare students to function at the peak of their potential in a multiracial, multicultural society. It is a mission in the pluralistic tradition that has marked the college since its beginnings as a seminary after the Civil War, educating Hungarians, Germans, Italians, and other ethnic groups, and that is still recognized in a covenant with the Synod of the Northeast Presbyterian Church (U.S.A.). That mission is shaped by, and serves, Bloomfield's current student body of 1,800 students, mostly from urban areas of New Jersey: approximately half men and half women; half traditional college age and half adults returning to school; 40 percent African American, 40 percent white, 10 percent Latino, and 10 percent international students, including great ethnic diversity within these larger groups. With such a mission, history, and profile, the college has been a good laboratory for change, a microcosm of the society to come (Levine and Associates, 1989), and a place for individual growth and institutional transformation.

Readiness for Change. As the demographics of the college shifted in the 1970s toward their current pluralism, faculty acted as "reflective practitioners" (Schön, 1983), meeting new teaching/learning situations with a "knowing-in-practice" that was intuitive, incorporating and transcending theories. But the needs of our students, our intellectual inquiry, and our focus on teaching demanded a more dramatic, unified, and coherent transformation.

Beginning in 1987, this transformation was orchestrated by a new president, John F. Noonan, who saw the college's multicultural identity as a unique resource and gave crucial support and leadership from the top (Wilkerson, 1992; Green, 1989; Yarbrough, 1992). He led the trustees and faculty to refocus the mission on students' potential and the diversity of the college and society. The distinctive mission helped to secure and direct resources for college-wide change.

Institution-Wide Approach. From 1989 to 1991 a major competitive grant from the New Jersey Department of Higher Education helped Bloomfield to expand key programs, create new ones, and link these in a unified project. "Toward a Multiracial, Multicultural Society" was Bloomfield College's Excellence Initiative for the Independents Project. It supported programs that reached every sector of the campus: students, faculty, administration, and staff. It supported programs for faculty and curriculum development, human relations, leadership and mentoring, honors, information technology, the arts-as-catalyst, and visiting minority scholars. The programs were dynamic—and still are, as they have been mainstreamed into the college, phased in to institutional and new outside funding, rather than phased out. College, foundation, and corporate funds now support these programs as well as retention programs that target at-risk populations.

Curricular Transformation Through Faculty Development. The Faculty and Curriculum Development Program has been central to collegiate change. Faculty development already had its own tradition and strong leadership at the college: a standing committee for development; annual three-day, on-campus faculty development conferences; individual projects focusing on teaching; and studies on student learning through class observation and interviews of students in the Master Faculty Program (Katz and Henry, 1988). The coordinator of Bloomfield's Teaching and Learning Center was for two years director of the statewide Master Faculty Program, and the college president is an author and editor on teaching minority students (Cones, Noonan, and Janha, 1983).

With this background, and believing that they could not give what they did not have, Bloomfield approached multicultural curriculum development through further faculty development (Green, 1989; Baker, 1983). Starting with the concrete goal to revise or develop one course, faculty restudied their disciplines for the content and perspectives of race, gender, ethnicity, and class. Their exploration and discussions led naturally to an infusion model, in which the whole of curriculum reflects multicultural reality and requires students to use multicultural perspectives in critical thinking (Gaff, 1992).

Each semester for five consecutive semesters a new group of about eight faculty volunteers started their year-long program. Each semester the director reviewed the preliminary list of participants, and recruited from academic disciplines not represented, and invited faculty leaders to create small groups who would influence further change (Rodgers, 1983).

Faculty worked together in a semester-long interdisciplinary seminar led by a preceptor in residence, an expert in issues of diversity from another institution. Readings for the seminars varied with the preceptor in residence and included educational research and theory, sociology, learning psychology, and history, as well as autobiographies and novels for direct experience of the voices and worldviews of different cultures. Dialogue in the seminar was tied to teaching, with faculty working collectively to solve common problems such as student apathy or weak preparation for academic or social demands (Gaff, 1992).

Simultaneously, faculty began a year of individual study with preceptors in their own disciplines, chosen for expertise in issues of diversity. In
general, preceptors provided bibliographies, guidance for study, and
scholarly dialogue. Some faculty met their preceptors weekly, others
monthly; a few chose to study independently.

Faculty then focused on curriculum revision in a week-long summer
workshop. They presented their own work in progress. They applied it to
course goals, class format and dynamics, collaborative learning, assignment construction, and evaluation methods (McKeachie, 1983; Bruffee,
1984; Smith and Kolb, 1986). Some faculty taught sample classes for peer
critiques. As the new or revised courses were taught, faculty observed
each other's courses and interviewed each other's students, a practice
based on the Master Faculty Program. This process gives faculty analysis
of the course in progress and peer support for the risk-taking that is part
of innovative teaching.

A Teaching and Learning Center was established to broaden faculty
development and, after the initial grant money expired, to continue
programming. The center sponsors weekly discussion groups, faculty
forums, and a newsletter of ideas and innovations.

Diverse Programs for Diversity. A network of programs saturate the
campus to reach multiple populations in varied ways. For example, the
Human Relations Program conducts workshops and multicultural events
and staff training; it particularly focuses on resident directors, resident
advisers, and dormitory students. An improvisational theater troupe
raises issues of pluralism, values, and decision making in and out of
classes. The Freshman Year Program is part of an academic support
system that targets at-risk students and dramatically increases retention.
Leadership Programs develop the skills of established and potential
student leaders. The Mentoring Program pairs students with mentors
who are leaders in business and their communities. Mentors provide
moral support, guidance, and opportunities to visit businesses and to
explore cultural activities. The Honors Program recognizes achievement
both through honor societies and annual awards ceremonies; the Arts-as-
Catalyst Program uses art, dance, theater, video, and circus to teach
diversity, trust, and communication in nontraditional ways. Diversity
also shapes programs for gallery exhibitions, visiting artists, special
workshops, writers' readings, and musicians' and dancers' performances.

The Visiting Minority Scholars Program helps us increase diversity in
the faculty and allows students to interact with people who represent a
variety of cultural perspectives (Green, 1989). Representation within
Bloomfield's full-time faculty has increased from about 3 percent in 1987
to 16 percent in 1991 to 23 percent in 1992.

Curricular and Institutional Evaluation and Transformation. Evaluation of Excellence Initiative programs was ongoing and carried out by

several means. All curricular programs were reviewed by faculty council and committees at the midpoint, goals were reaffirmed, and revisions were made. A consultant observed the faculty seminar every semester, noting its character and evolution. For individual programs and for the project as a whole, focus groups were conducted of students and of faculty. Our institutional self-study questionnaire of students had sections on multicultural education and the mission of the college. An external review panel of national leaders visited once a year.

The impact of the Faculty and Curriculum Development Program has been broad. Over half of the full-time faculty, plus twenty adjuncts and administrators who teach, went through the program. Faculty found that multicultural education did not need to become just another "ism." Most faculty evolved two distinct, complementary meanings for multicultural education. One is based on academic criteria: students develop critical thinking using a multicultural perspective with reference to their own and other backgrounds, and with materials from within and without the traditional canon. The other definition has social and experiential components: a multicultural education means becoming familiar with and appreciating diversity among students and the larger community (Hochwald, 1991a, 1991b). Faculty found inclusive material and methods to be intellectually sound and renewing, the traditional canon to be enriched by multicultural perspectives, and the debates about diversity to be themselves subjects for classroom discussion. Their revisions affected the freshman and sophomore cores; courses in the humanities, social and behavioral sciences, nursing, natural science, math, business, accounting, and economics; tutoring and developmental courses; workshops and services in academic support and student affairs; and library services and collections.

Survey and genre courses include the contributions and perspectives of individuals and groups outside the mainstream. Examples: "Western Civilization" is now taught "in World Perspective." American literature and art courses include artists, writers, and scholarship from underrepresented groups. Sociology includes multicultural content and examines biases from previously excluded perspectives. Developmental mathematics is taught with sensitivity to culturally influenced learning styles and with word problems that reflect the environments students know. Genetics includes research on values in science, for example, in intelligence testing and color heredity. American history courses focus on social history. Tutors are trained to deal with varied learning styles. In library and arts programming, diversity is the norm. Some faculty report that not only curriculum and pedagogy but they themselves have changed. Foreign-born faculty report new understandings of American race and ethnicity. Many faculty and staff report new openness concerning students' lives and the expectations they bring to college (Yarbrough, 1992).

More faculty are using collaborative learning, are conscious of giving students context for new material, and see that issues of diversity can affect teaching in any discipline, even accounting, computing, genetics, or mathematics.

Infusion of multicultural content and perspectives is ongoing. The General Education Committee confirms the importance of multicultural education in its goals for a revised program. Faculty's focus on teaching, course revisions, and the work of the General Education Committee have now focused us on holistic assessment.

The student questionnaire shows that almost 90 percent of respondents believe that they are getting a multicultural education, that the faculty are dedicated to providing it, and that the students will be better prepared professionally and personally on graduation because of it.

What helped us succeed? It was crucial to make faculty development interdisciplinary and community-wide. The staggered start-up schedule accommodated faculty's availability, initiated the program with enthusiastic faculty who became ambassadors, and built an ever-increasing cohort focused on multicultural issues. The length and sequence allowed faculty time to reflect, to have a sustained dialogue with their colleagues, to make lasting change, and to model lifelong learning (White, 1980). The goal to start by revising one course attracted faculty to the program; however, they report that their studies affected their pedagogy and thus all of their courses; content changed in many courses, not only the one targeted for revision. Some faculty followed their work in the seminar with expanded research (an oral history project, for example, or research on Islam in New Jersey).

Faculty shaped and owned the program. No one presented a checklist for revising a syllabus; academic freedom was assured. Having an "outsider" as preceptor in residence brought new perspectives and meant the seminar's leader was without ties to other campus agendas.

Dissemination was a new opportunity for development. Faculty were included in proposals for presenting the program as a model with their studies, curriculum, and pedagogy as outcomes. At local and national conferences, the response of colleagues from other institutions showed faculty the context and value of their accomplishments, and they returned to this small college with additional pride and sense of renewal.

There evolved an interdisciplinary community of teachers who came to know each other through studying together and sharing their hopes and frustrations. They raised their expectations of students and felt more able to take risks: to "teach with courage," in the words of one preceptor.

The enhancement of community is also the result of the programs that support student development and affect campus climate. Our multifaceted approach has created a new atmosphere and energy at the college; it has brought us both exhilaration and exhaustion. We make no claim of complete success in any area. The challenge of preparing students to function in a multiracial, multicultural society is ongoing. The challenge to build community from diversity is ongoing.

St. Norbert College

Leadership. A year after taking office as St. Norbert's fifth president, Thomas A. Manion directed a broad-based planning committee to study the future size and composition of the student body. He was primarily concerned about the homogeneity of the students, since there were fewer than ten American students from underrepresented groups in an enrollment of more than 1,700. The committee recommended that by 1990 multicultural and international students make up 6 percent of the enrollment.

The skepticism of the older faculty was based on memories of failure. In the late 1960s the college vigorously recruited African American and other students from underrepresented groups. Almost 100 percent dropped out before graduation. But there were also a few successes: Charles Holton remembers being the only black student when he arrived in 1947, the same year that Jackie Robinson broke into major league baseball. As he confronted each personal challenge, he asked himself "What would Jackie do?" The inspiration of Jackie Robinson got him through to graduation four years later. James Flowers had a similar experience when he arrived on campus in 1965, the recipient of a scholarship funded by a faculty member. Four years later he went to Harvard and MIT, where he achieved both an M.D. and Ph.D. Likewise, a small number of Menominees and Oneidas attended and graduated.

By the 1980s, however, a large number of new faculty had replaced those who took advantage of a new phased retirement program. Many of these individuals felt that diversity was a moral and educational imperative, and accepted the president's challenge to try again.

Menominee tribal officials presented the first opportunity to the faculty. In 1986, they met with the St. Norbert director of teacher education, "Father Tom," a Norbertine priest who joined the faculty in 1984 as a result of a midlife career change. The Menominee tribe of Wisconsin has a 220,000-acre reservation located about fifty miles from the campus. Menominees make up almost 100 percent of the enrollment in their school district, in which 90 percent of faculty and staff are non-Indians. They asked St. Norbert to form a partnership with them to design a special program that would produce thirty-five degreed and certified Menominees in five years. They would assist with the funding.

After discussing this proposition with the academic dean and his colleagues, Father Tom invited several faculty members (representing all three divisions) to lunch. He outlined the Menominee request, which included scheduling the first two years of course work on the reservation, inaugurating a Menominee Studies minor, and providing tutoring, counseling, and developmental courses as required.

The faculty response was dramatic. In fact, the meeting had the tenor of an awakening or religious revival. In a three-month period the faculty designed the curriculum and program, and all the key committees gave their approval. It was quite a challenge, since the college had no prior experience in extended studies. The faculty insisted that they would staff the off-campus courses with the best full-time members including senior professors.

Once the new project was funded, St. Norbert College and Menominee officials developed several mechanisms to promote dialogue and to build mutual trust and understanding. For instance, the tribe invited college faculty for a "day-long get-acquainted," which included tours, meetings with tribal members, and a meal. A busload went. It was the first time many had set foot on an Indian reservation. During the next two years, fifteen faculty members had the experience of teaching at Keshena, and most found the experience very positive.

Chronologically, the next step was development of precollege programs that enabled St. Norbert and the Native American communities to get used to each other. Between 1987 and 1989, faculty and staff members in education, mathematics, and leadership studies won grant funding and developed a variety of summer programs for underrepresented students. The largest began as a partnership with the Oneida Tribe (which is located about ten miles from campus) and now includes a large number of Hmong and Laotian youth from the region also. The most ambitious is a residential summer math and science enrichment program that attracts students nationally. These programs involve a large number of St. Norbert faculty members in program design and teaching, and the experience has also been positive.

Community-Wide Involvement. It was now time to move beyond special programs and institutionalize opportunities for diverse students. An African American student took the initiative. After discussing his plans with key college officials, he convened an ad hoc committee to prepare a diversity plan. The committee attracted students, faculty, and administrators, as well as members of the noncampus community. During a two-year period they met regularly to discuss plans and to experiment with ideas. At the conclusion of the second year, they submitted "Pastoral Vision" to the administration.

Pastoral Vision was a comprehensive document that spelled out the actions necessary for attracting and retaining diverse students. The recommendations touched on admission, student services, library resources, financial aid, community relations, and many other important factors. The final recommendation was that the college establish an office of multicultural affairs and hire a full-time person to supervise implementation of the Pastoral Vision. In December 1989, the first director of multicultural affairs took office. Despite some rough spots during the first eighteen months, diversity did show some gains on campus. The director organized many types of cultural and educational events, including performances, lectures, and debates. By the fall of 1991, enrollment of underrepresented students had increased to fifty-eight—an increase from .6 percent to 3 percent. At the same time the college also increased enrollment of international students.

External Funding. The expense of attending a private college full-time presents a formidable barrier to many students from underrepresented groups. St. Norbert provides more than $6 million in funding for grants, scholarships, and work study. Early on, college officials understood the need to establish scholarships for its Menominee partners. A New York foundation seeded a new scholarship endowment, and local donors have added to it. Since then donors have established scholarships for members of other underrepresented groups. These scholarships meet a real financial need while also signifying college commitment.

In January 1991, the Lilly Endowment of Indiana presented an opportunity to the college. They issued a request for proposals in a new program designed to improve the campus climate for diversity. They would not fund direct recruitment. Members of the new standing faculty committee on cultural diversity, administrators appointed by the president, and students came together to develop a proposal. They met regularly from January to May. The Lilly Endowment funded the application effective in December 1991.

Faculty, Staff, and Trustee Development. The proposal began where Pastoral Vision left off, with a major component devoted to activities leading to the appointment of faculty members from underrepresented groups. The grant funds a paired college program, visiting scholars, and graduate fellows. St. Norbert College faculty and staff work closely with a historically black college, a tribal community college, and a socially diverse Chicago urban college. In other programs, visiting scholars and graduate fellows from underrepresented groups provide greater visibility in teaching roles. In the process of recruiting for these positions, academic leaders build networks they need in order to recruit candidates for full-time tenure slots. The grant also establishes summer stipends for faculty who wish to modify existing courses or create new, more inclusive courses.

Grant planners assumed that members of the St. Norbert community lacked the knowledge and experience to deal comfortably with students from underrepresented groups. Therefore the grant permitted the college to send faculty and staff to a training workshop with the National Coalition Building Institute that led to on-campus training of trainers and on-campus workshops. These workshops foster an appreciation of diversity and help build and foster community. The faculty developed their own plans to improve campus climate in support of diversity, beginning with a voluntary off-campus retreat and leading to a faculty action plan. Finally, a trustee and task force retreat, having analyzed demographics and the implications for college enrollment in the next decade, concluded that St. Norbert must diversify further or accept a smaller enrollment, and that a greater diversity of students was essential for educational reasons as well, to prepare all St. Norbert students to live and work in an increasingly diverse society (Hodgkinson, 1990a, 1990b; Mingle and Rodriguez, 1990; Education Commission of the States, 1990).

The campus has recently welcomed a new associate dean for cultural diversity. She has been active across the campus and in the community. A milestone occurred when the Faculty Development Committee invited her to join them in planning the annual faculty conference, which brought together thirty-five African American, Hispanic, and Hmong and Native American citizens and leaders for dialogue with the faculty. Panels included students from diverse backgrounds talking about their problems as well as their dreams and concluded with a meal at which the Hmong presented traditional dances and songs.

Enrollment projections are positive and include efforts of admission officials, who had supported diversity objectives, but now mount special programs focused on underrepresented populations. They have connected with African American groups in Milwaukee, Native Americans locally, and Hmong community groups throughout northeastern and central Wisconsin. For instance, planners for a black student college night in Milwaukee requested St. Norbert to conduct a college planning workshop. The Hmong community in Green Bay asked for a similar workshop and provided an interpreter so that parents could also be involved.

Conclusion

An advantage of a small private college is its ability to change rapidly. The deliberative academic process usually slows change, but members of a small college are not limited by the bureaucracies that public sector educators face. At St. Norbert and Bloomfield alike, administrators, faculty members, and community people all seized the initiative at various times. The result has been a dramatic and comprehensive movement to institutionalize diversity.

References

Baker, G. C. *Planning and Organizing for Multicultural Instruction.* Reading, Mass.: Addison-Wesley, 1983.

Bruffee, K. A. "Collaborative Writing and the 'Conversation of Mankind.'" *College English,* 1984, *46,* 635–652.

Cones, J.J.H., Noonan, J. F., Janha, D. (eds.). *Teaching Minority Students.* New Directions for Teaching and Learning, no. 16. San Francisco: Jossey-Bass, 1983.

Education Commission of the States. *Achieving Campus Diversity: Policies for Change.* Denver, Colo.: Education Commission of the States, 1990.

Gaff, J. "Beyond Politics: The Educational Issues Inherent in Multicultural Education." *Change,* 1992, *24* (1), 30–36.

Green, M. F. *Minorities on Campus: A Handbook for Enhancing Diversity.* Washington, D.C.: American Council on Education, 1989.

Hochwald, E. *Spring 1991 Faculty Development Seminar on Multiculturalism.* Unpublished report, Associate Dean for Academic Affairs. Bloomfield, N.J.: Bloomfield College, 1991a.

Hochwald, E. *Focus Group Reports: Students and the Multicultural Curriculum, Faculty Development Seminar.* Unpublished reports, Associate Dean for Academic Affairs. Bloomfield, N.J.: Bloomfield College, 1991b.

Hodgkinson, H. L. *The Demographics of American Indians: One Percent of the People; Fifty Percent of the Diversity.* Washington, D.C.: Institute for Educational Leadership/Center for Demographic Policy, 1990a.

Hodgkinson, H. L. "Hard Numbers, Tough Choices." In *Association of Governing Boards of Colleges and Universities Reports,* Nov./Dec. 1990b, pp. 12–13, 16–17.

Katz, J., and Henry, M. *Turning Professors into Teachers: A New Approach to Faculty Development and Student Learning.* New York: American Council on Education/Macmillan, 1988.

Levine, A., and Associates. *Shaping Higher Education's Future: Demographic Realities and Opportunities, 1990–2000.* San Francisco: Jossey-Bass, 1989.

McKeachie, W. J. *Teaching Tips: A Guidebook for the Beginning College Teacher.* (8th ed.) Lexington, Mass.: Heath, 1983.

Mingle, J. R., and Rodriguez, E. M. (eds.). *Building Coalitions for Minority Success: A Report of the SHEEO Project on Minority Achievement in Higher Education.* Denver, Colo.: State Higher Education Executive Officers, 1990.

Rodgers, F. M. *Diffusion of Innovations.* (3rd ed.) New York: Free Press, 1983.

Schön, D. A. *The Reflective Practitioner: How Professionals Think in Action.* New York: Basic Books, 1983.

Smith, D. M., and Kolb, D. A. *User's Guide for the Learning Style Inventory.* Boston, Mass.: McBer, 1986.

White, A. M. "Developing and Challenging Faculty Through Interdisciplinary Teaching/Learning." In W. C. Nelson and M. E. Weigel (eds.), *Effective Approaches to Faculty Development.* Washington, D.C.: Association of American Colleges, 1980.

Wilkerson, M. B. "Beyond the Graveyard. Engaging Faculty Development." *Change,* 1992, *24* (1), 59–63.

Yarbrough, L. "Three Questions for the Multiculturalism Debate." *Change,* 1992, *24* (1), 64–69.

Martha J. LaBare is associate dean for academic affairs at Bloomfield College in Bloomfield, New Jersey.

Stuart G. Lang is executive director for Institutional Advancement and acting director of the International Center at St. Norbert College in De Pere, Wisconsin.

INDEX

ORDERING INFORMATION

NEW DIRECTIONS FOR TEACHING AND LEARNING is a series of paperback books that presents ideas and techniques for improving college teaching, based both on the practical expertise of seasoned instructors and on the latest research findings of educational and psychological researchers. Books in the series are published quarterly in Spring, Summer, Fall, and Winter and are available for purchase by subscription as well as by single copy.

SUBSCRIPTIONS for 1992 cost $45.00 for individuals (a savings of 20 percent over single-copy prices) and $60.00 for institutions, agencies, and libraries. Please do not send institutional checks for personal subscriptions. Standing orders are accepted.

SINGLE COPIES cost $14.95 when payment accompanies order. (California, New Jersey, New York, and Washington, D.C., residents please include appropriate sales tax.) Billed orders will be charged postage and handling.

DISCOUNTS FOR QUANTITY ORDERS are available. Please write to the address below for information.

ALL ORDERS must include either the name of an individual or an official purchase order number. Please submit your order as follows:
    Subscriptions: specify series and year subscription is to begin
    Single copies: include individual title code (such as TL1)

MAIL ALL ORDERS TO:
    Jossey-Bass Publishers
    350 Sansome Street
    San Francisco, California 94104

FOR SALES OUTSIDE OF THE UNITED STATES CONTACT:
    Maxwell Macmillan International Publishing Group
    866 Third Avenue
    New York, New York 10022

U.S. Postal Service

STATEMENT OF OWNERSHIP, MANAGEMENT AND CIRCULATION
Required by 39 U.S.C. 3685

1A. Title of Publication	1B. PUBLICATION NO.	2. Date of Filing
NEW DIRECTIONS FOR TEACHING AND LEARNING	0 0 1 – 8 0 1	10/16/92

3. Frequency of Issue	3A. No. of Issues Published Annually	3B. Annual Subscription Price
Quarterly	Four (4)	$45 (individual) $60 (institutional)

4. Complete Mailing Address of Known Office of Publication *(Street, City, County, State and ZIP+4 Code) (Not printers)*

350 Sansome Street, San Francisco, CA 94104-1310

5. Complete Mailing Address of the Headquarters of General Business Offices of the Publisher *(Not printer)*

(above address)

6. Full Names and Complete Mailing Address of Publisher, Editor, and Managing Editor *(This item MUST NOT be blank)*

Publisher *(Name and Complete Mailing Address)*

Jossey-Bass Inc., Publishers (above address)

Editor *(Name and Complete Mailing Address)*

Robert J. Menges, Northwestern University, Center for the Teaching Professions, 2003 Sheridan Road, Evanston, IL 60208-2610

Managing Editor *(Name and Complete Mailing Address)*

Lynn Luckow, President, Jossey-Bass Inc., Publishers

7. Owner *(If owned by a corporation, its name and address must be stated and also immediately thereunder the names and addresses of stockholders owning or holding 1 percent or more of total amount of stock. If not owned by a corporation, the names and addresses of the individual owners must be given. If owned by a partnership or other unincorporated firm, its name and address, as well as that of each individual must be given. If the publication is published by a nonprofit organization, its name and address must be stated.) (Item must be completed.)*

Full Name	Complete Mailing Address
Maxwell Communications Corp., plc	Headington Hill Hall Oxford OX30BW U.K.

8. Known Bondholders, Mortgagees, and Other Security Holders Owning or Holding 1 Percent or More of Total Amount of Bonds, Mortgages or Other Securities *(If there are none, so state)*

Full Name	Complete Mailing Address
same as above	same as above

9. For Completion by Nonprofit Organizations Authorized To Mail at Special Rates *(DMM Section 423.12 only)*
The purpose, function, and nonprofit status of this organization and the exempt status for Federal income tax purposes *(Check one)*

(1) ☐ Has Not Changed During Preceding 12 Months	(2) ☐ Has Changed During Preceding 12 Months	*If changed, publisher must submit explanation of change with this statement.*

10. Extent and Nature of Circulation *(See instructions on reverse side)*	Average No. Copies Each Issue During Preceding 12 Months	Actual No. Copies of Single Issue Published Nearest to Filing Date
A. Total No. Copies *(Net Press Run)*	1800	1857
B. Paid and/or Requested Circulation 1. Sales through dealers and carriers, street vendors and counter sales	187	31
2. Mail Subscription *(Paid and/or requested)*	835	892
C. Total Paid and/or Requested Circulation *(Sum of 10B1 and 10B2)*	1022	923
D. Free Distribution by Mail, Carrier or Other Means Samples, Complimentary, and Other Free Copies	99	100
E. Total Distribution *(Sum of C and D)*	1121	1023
F. Copies Not Distributed 1. Office use, left over, unaccounted, spoiled after printing	679	834
2. Return from News Agents	-0-	-0-
G. TOTAL *(Sum of E, F1 and 2—should equal net press run shown in A)*	1800	1857

11. I certify that the statements made by me above are correct and complete	Signature and Title of Editor, Publisher, Business Manager, or Owner *(signature)* Larry Ishii Vice-President

PS Form 3526, Feb. 1989   *(See instructions on reverse)*